The Prayer of Freedom™

God's *breakthrough* plan to free you from chronic health issues, anxiety, depression, addictions, and other life challenges

D1546052

by
Beatty Carmichael

for additional copies, go to:
www.**ThePrayerOfFreedom*Book*.com**

Published by Maran Ministries LLC

The Prayer of Freedom (vs 3.01 – 231020)
Copyright © 2023 Beatty Carmichael

Unless otherwise noted, all scriptures are from ESV. Scripture quotations marked **ESV** are from The ESV® Bible (The Holy Bible, English Standard Version®), copyright © 2001 by Crossway, a publishing ministry of Good News Publishers. Used by permission. All rights reserved.

Scripture quotations marked **NIV** are taken from the Holy Bible, New International Version®, NIV®. Copyright © 1973, 1978, 1984, 2011 by Biblica, Inc.™ Used by permission of Zondervan. All rights reserved worldwide. www.zondervan.com. The "NIV" and "New International Version" are trademarks registered in the United States Patent and Trademark Office by Biblica, Inc.™

Scripture quotations marked **NLT** are from the Holy Bible, New Living Translation, Copyright © 1996, 2004, 2015 by Tyndale House Foundation. Used by permission of Tyndale House Publishers, Inc., Carol Stream, Illinois 60188. All rights reserved.

Scripture quotations marked **TLB** are from The Living Bible copyright © 1971. Used by permission of Tyndale House Publishers, Carol Stream, Illinois 60188. All rights reserved.

ISBN: 979-8-9890591-0-2

TABLE OF CONTENTS

Section 1 — What's Going On?

Section 2 — The Prayer and Next Steps

Appendix

ABOUT THIS BOOK

I've seen people set free from arthritis; I've seen the same with glaucoma, broken hips, addictions, and so much more. I've even seen parent-child and marriage problems start recovering because of this prayer...

———————————

The Prayer of Freedom is a specific approach to prayer that gives people breakthrough from many of life's most challenging issues. **Mental issues** such as anxiety, depression, panic attacks, bipolar disorder, and PTSD. Chronic **health issues** such as asthma, fibromyalgia, and arthritis. And even **personal issues** such as relationship friction, addictions, and more.

The secret to the prayer is when you follow God's laws, he intervenes and helps restore your life.

To illustrate, here are the results of a survey I did with the Prayer of Freedom...

I do volunteer teaching at an addiction recovery center. As you might imagine, these people are dealing with all kinds of issues in their lives — addictions, depression, anxiety, bipolar disorder, anger issues, abuse, trauma, and much more. While preparing to write this book, I wanted to statistically measure how effective this prayer was, so I did a survey with them.

I had each person in my classes make a list of issues they were dealing with in their lives, then rate each issue on an intensity scale to indicate how bad it was. Next, I had them do the Prayer of Freedom. Once they did, they updated me on what happened in their lives. Here's what their data showed...

Nearly 9 out of 10 (<u>90% of those surveyed</u>) re-ceived *significant* relief from their issues, while the remaining 1 out of 10 reported only minimal relief.

Of the 90% who received significant relief, here's a deeper look at their results. Now keep in mind, these people had *a lot* of issues going on in their lives, much more than your average person. Most of them had been abused or abandoned, many had lived on the streets, and most had been living with multiple addictions and all the associated issues that come along with them for years.

Even with the accumulation of all these problems, all but one saw almost *all* of their issues completely dis-appear — **100% relief of everything** from mental tor-ment (heaviness, depression, bipolar disorder, anxi-ety); addiction urges (for drugs, alcohol, pornography, and sex); and all kinds of physical issues like chronic health and pain problems they had been suffering with for years. All of it... *gone!*

And it's not just personal issues like those that it helps with. I've also seen it help with constant job fail-ures, marital and personal relationships, and more.

I remember when a friend and his family came to visit from out of town. He and his wife were always bickering, and all of the affection had left their mar-riage years ago. On top of that, their eight year old daughter was always "hyper fidgety" and was con-stantly wearing them out.

My friend and I talked long into the night about both of these issues. I then led him in the Prayer of Freedom. He prayed through it, asked the Lord to inter-vene, then went to bed.

The next day, there were *significant* changes. For the first time in years, his wife was actually friendly and affectionate towards him. While watching their daughter on the rope swing, his wife snuggled up against him and tenderly rubbed his back. There was no bickering, no accusing... just a pleasant time enjoying being together as a family. And the daughter — she was still an active eight year old, but the "hyper fidgety" part was gone. It made a huge difference on the rest of the weekend

So, how does this prayer work?

It simply taps into God's spiritual laws as laid out in the Bible. And when you follow his laws, he brings the relief!

In this book, you'll learn about these spiritual laws and how to apply them in your life through this very specific approach to prayer. Additionally, I share amazing stories of what God has done in many peoples' lives. Stories that seem unbelievable until you understand how God's spiritual laws actually work.

If *you* suffer from chronic health or pain issues, relationship issues, mental or psychological issues, or even career and job related issues, then based on what I've seen you likely have a 90% chance to get free of them with the Prayer of Freedom!

And the great part about it is, not only does it work when you pray it for yourself, it can also work when you pray it on behalf of a loved one — a child, spouse, or parent. It's very powerful.

So, if I've caught your attention, turn to **Chapter 1 and start reading it now.** It only takes eight minutes for the average reader, and you'll be amazed with what you learn.

ACKNOWLEDGMENTS

This book was born of a passion to serve the Lord and to set his people free. It would not have been possible were it not for a number of people who were instrumental in helping bring this book to reality.

First is **my wife, PA,** who helped me these last seven years as the Lord trained and instructed me in the precepts behind the Prayer of Freedom.

Second is **Eric Schrag**, my editor, without whom this book would not be the amazing work that it is. It carries his "DNA" as much as it does mine, and it was his tireless efforts that make it so easy to understand.

Third is **Phyllis Tarbox** of Above and Beyond Christian Counseling, who greatly clarified many technical aspects pertaining to sin and repentance. She also shared a systematic approach of repentance prayers that ultimately led to the Prayer of Freedom.

Fourth is **Ken Fish** of Orbis Ministries. Though we've never officially met, his teachings related to "agreement sins" (my term) and secret societies were influential in making a critical portion of this prayer possible.

And fifth is a host of others, including **Father Spotswood** and **Sydney Petite**, who helped bring into sharper focus many aspects instrumental in setting people free.

To all of you, I thank the Lord that he brought you into my life, and I thank you for your crucial contributions to this work!

INTRODUCTION

Seven years ago, as I'm writing this, the Lord placed a burden on my heart to help set people free.

I guess you could say it was in my blood. I come from a line of seven generations of medical doctors, people in whose heart was the desire to set others free from infirmities. Even though I never became a doctor myself, the Lord placed the same mantle upon me to set people free that he placed upon my family for generations. And, seven years ago, he revealed it to me.

It started with a deep desire to help people get free of infirmities. The Lord began showing me how to pray for them, and I began seeing incredible results. Then, a year later, he expanded the types of issues I would pray for to include other life challenges as well.

While it fascinated me, it frustrated me at the same time. I often felt "defeated" when I couldn't help people get free. So, I began taking more of a scientific approach to my praying. I asked the Lord for wisdom, then began testing things I felt he was showing me. I would test, pray with people, and measure the results.

Over the years, I started seeing a definite pattern. If people repented of specific sins *before* I prayed with them, many more were set free from their issues.

The Lord then placed other people in my path who taught me more about the spiritual laws at play. And almost all of those laws revolved around sin. That's when I realized the root of most of these issues was sin, and the solution was repentance.

During this time, the Lord blessed me with amazing teaching opportunities that few get to experience. The most surreal of these was allowing me several times to actually *speak* with what I call "spirits of discipline" (these are spirits tied to unrepented sin). From these "interviews" I began to better understand their role and the impact unrepented sins play in it. Those were experiences I'll never forget!

Then, over the years following that, I began seeing a pattern form from all of this. That pattern was simple...

Sins give spirits of discipline a right to "torment" you. Repenting of those sins voided those rights. Once voided, the Lord would remove them when you asked him to. And when they left, the issues stopped.

It was a simple revelation, but it took years to fully recognize it and grasp how to use that knowledge to consistently help people get breakthrough.

In addition to this, I began seeing a pattern of how to pray with people that would set them free. From there, I systematized the prayer process — how to identify the right sins, how to repent of them, and how to ask the Lord to remove the spirits of discipline.

And that was the birth of the Prayer of Freedom!

As I started testing it, I saw astoundingly consistent results. So much so that I realized I was "on to something," as the saying goes. I saw people set free from arthritis; I saw the same with glaucoma, broken hips, addictions, and so much more. I've even seen parent-child and marriage problems start recovering because of this prayer.

So, going back to my testing regimen, I began doing surveys with those who had extreme issues in life. I found that nearly 9 out of 10 who did the Prayer of Freedom received nearly **100% relief** of most, if not all, of their issues!

When I stepped back and looked at this from afar, I realized it was nothing new. This was in the Bible all the time — the secret had simply been hiding in plain sight.

Jesus said he came to give us abundant life. And the primary message he preached was simple: "repent!"

If we simply did what he commands us to do, there'd be no need for the Prayer of Freedom, because that's all it really is. It's a simple way to repent of sins, then ask God to remove the issues in your life and give you the abundant life he promised. And he does!

So, that's the message you'll see in this book. You'll also read a lot of stories of people that illustrate how it works. And while these stories may come across as too good to be true, I assure you they are all real. The only thing *not* real about them is I changed the names to protect their privacy.

I pray the Prayer of Freedom blesses you as much as it has blessed countless others.

Beatty Carmichael

P.S. This book is a simplified teaching on the topic of spiritual warfare. If you want a more complete understanding on spiritual warfare, watch my video teaching at GetRadicalFaith.com/SpiritualWarfare.

FOR MY BIBLE SCHOLAR FRIENDS

Because the underlying foundation of this book is a highly complex, theological topic, I want to take a moment to share *how* this book was written. This may be helpful for my Bible scholar friends.

As you read this book, it's important to keep in mind two key things I'm focused on. First, my audience is average people who are not theologically trained. And second, my objective is to move them to *do* the Prayer of Freedom, not to teach the full, theological premises behind the prayer. Because of these focuses, I've embraced two key tenets while writing this book...

▶ Simplicity over precision

The first tenet is simplicity over precision.

Whenever you simplify a complex subject, you will always lose precision. And if you've been trained to be theologically precise, you'll likely see instances where I am less theologically precise than I could be.

However, since my objective is to teach *why* to do the Prayer of Freedom rather than the theology behind it, I have greatly simplified, and even generalized at times, certain aspects of this book to the point of being theologically imprecise.

It's similar to what Jesus did when teaching his disciples the Parable of the Unmerciful Servant that I discuss in Chapter 4.

In that parable, Jesus teaches on the consequences one will receive if he doesn't forgive others. But one could almost say his teaching is theologically *imprecise*. Why? Because it's done in the form of a parable, and parables only give shadows of truths, not the full precision of those truths.

But his objective wasn't to be theologically precise; it was only to be precise *enough* to teach his disciples *why* they should forgive (so their heavenly Father wouldn't turn them over to the jailer to be tortured (**Matthew 18:34-35**)).

In a similar way, I have simplified certain aspects in this book to such a degree that they, too, are theologically imprecise. They are only precise *enough* to teach my readers *why* they should repent (so they can be set free from their issues).

▶ Statements over explanations

To keep this book shorter, I also embraced making statements rather than giving explanations when the full explanation isn't crucial to my objective. Most statements I make are supported in Scripture; others are from experiences I have observed over the years.

If you have questions regarding the scriptural accuracy of some of these statements, please review my full teaching on this subject where I cover the Biblical references in more detail. You can find this teaching at GetRadicalFaith.com/SpiritualWarfare.

What if you disagree with my theology?

The approach of the Prayer of Freedom is simple: repent of sins the Lord brings to your mind, then ask him to remove certain issues from your life, and he will. The outcome of this approach has been so consistent it is *undisputable* that this prayer works.

However, in terms of the theology behind *why* it works, I must admit I don't fully understand all of God's truths. In fact, I'm confident I understand far *less* than 1% of them (my guess is you'd probably admit the same about yourself).

Because of that, it's hard for me to be too dogmatic about whether I've "nailed it" in terms of the theology behind *why* this prayer works. However, my theological belief on why it works isn't nearly as important as the fact that it *does* work. And as you read this book, I encourage you to stay focused on that.

Jeremiah 28:9 says (paraphrased), "If a prophet's prediction comes true, it is proof he was sent by the Lord." So, if you end up disagreeing with my theology behind this prayer (Section 1), please don't reject the prayer itself (Section 2).

My hope is you will have enough confidence from the stories I share and the surveys I've done to accept the fact that this prayer *might* actually work. And because it is easy enough to verify, I challenge you to put it to the test and let the Lord prove it true or not.

Since the prayer's entire focus is repenting of sins for which the Lord prompts you, then asking him to remove issues from your life, there are NO repercussions. If it doesn't work, the only thing you'll have done is repent of sins... and that *always* pleases the Lord. So, there is no downside and no risk.

And if you are a pastor, because of the *significant* impact the Prayer of Freedom could have on your congregation, I hope you'll see enough importance for their sake to at least test it.

Here's a simple way you can do a test. Get at least five members from your congregation who struggle with various issues — depression, anxiety, chronic pain or health problems, addictions, etc. Have them go through the prayer as I outline in Section 2. Then tabulate their results.

I'm certain you will be *amazed* by what God does. And once you see what happens, you'll start seeing all kinds of ways this prayer can impact others in your congregation!

– Section 1 –

What's Going On?

Chapter 1

God's spiritual laws of discipline and breakthrough

Penny grew up in a normal, Christian home. Her parents took her to church every Sunday, and she tried to live right to the best of her ability.

As we were talking one day, she shared that all through high school and college she had been healthy, never sick, and had remained a virgin. But then, she started dating a boy in college, and three weeks before graduation she gave herself to him and slept with him.

"What happened next was the beginning of a health nightmare," she said. "Within a few weeks, I got sick... and *stayed* sick for nearly twenty years!"

First, there was a car accident with a broken vertebra in her neck. Then, there was strep throat. Later, she was diagnosed with toxic shock. Then, she had strep throat a second time. Next, she was diagnosed with precancerous cells and underwent surgery to remove them. She became an alcoholic and life continued spiraling downward. After that, she had several bronchial infections, strep throat for a third time... a fourth, fifth, sixth and even seventh time!

At that point, she started living on antibiotics to try and combat all her sicknesses. During this time, she began suffering from constant joint and muscle pain, and the doctors finally diagnosed her as having Chronic Fatigue and Fibromyalgia... with no cure.

That's when a friend guided her through the same process as the Prayer of Freedom. Penny repented of her sins — not just sleeping with her boyfriend, but others she had accumulated throughout the years — and asked God to remove her issues.

"Within one day," she said, "*all* my sickness and addiction disappeared! No more fatigue, no more pain, no more stiffness in my limbs, no more strep throat, no more urge to drink — it was all gone!"

Fast forward to today...

"That was twenty years ago," Penny said, "and I am still free today. *None* of the sicknesses have returned, and I haven't had another drink since, either."

Her doctors claimed it was a "miracle." But it wasn't a miracle; she simply did what the Lord said to do — she repented of her sins. And when she did, he released her from the consequence of those sins.

"Wait, hold on a moment!" you might be exclaiming. "Are you trying to say her illnesses were due to *sin*?"

Yes. That's exactly what I'm saying. Although not *all* illnesses are tied to sin, many are. And not just illnesses, but a lot more of all the issues we go through in life. And what I'm about to share with you, *directly* from God's word, will transform your life.

And while you may not be like Penny, can you relate to what she went through? Do you have friends or loved ones experiencing similar issues?

Would you believe me if I told you this is all part of God's plan?

Wait... what?! At this point, you're probably ready to stop reading and storm out of the room. Maybe you're thinking to yourself, "This guy's crazy! How could this be part of God's plan? The God I believe in loves me. He wouldn't want me to suffer."

If that's you, I totally understand. But don't throw the book away just yet. Please hear me out. What I'm about to share might just transform the way you think... and change your life in "miraculous" ways, as it has for so many others!

So, why would a loving God allow you — or my friend Penny — to suffer with so many issues?

It's because God *does* love you!

Let me explain...

God's plan is to give YOU abundant life

It's all part of a plan God put in place since the beginning of creation. And it has to do with his spiritual laws of discipline and our means of breakthrough.

As most of us travel through life, we look at our earthly circumstances with earthly eyes, trying to figure out the cause-and-effect of what we did that might be causing our problems. We try to make sense of what goes on around us... and most of the time, we can't. So we end up living a life full of struggles and frustration, with no way out.

But the good news is you *can* be completely free of the darkness and heaviness in your life. You can be free of relationship challenges, constant life failures, or physical issues. And not only can you be free, but many of those problems can even be reversed. All it takes is the simple Prayer of Freedom.

Is a life like that really possible?

Yes, it is! I've been living it for years, and have helped numerous others move in that direction as well!

However, if you've never experienced it yourself, it's hard to comprehend what is possible. "Normal" for many people feels like the "thief" has always been stealing, killing, and destroying their lives. And if you've never known anything *but* that, it's hard to imagine how things can be any different. But that's what you're about to learn in this book — the simple steps God put in place for *you* to achieve freedom.

While sharing this with a small group of people one day, I explained it this way...

Imagine a child who has grown up in a broken, dysfunctional home. If that's all he's ever known, he has no clue other kids may actually live in happy, healthy families. Because he has no "grid" for it himself, he can't even understand what that would be like.

The same thing happens in our lives. Because we only see our earthly circumstances through our earthly eyes, that's all we know as reality. And for many of us, that reality is greatly lacking.

But that's not the reality God has for us. He said, "The thief comes to steal, kill, and destroy, but I came that you might have life, and have it *abundantly*." (**John 10:10**, paraphrased)

Unfortunately, many of us have no clue what an abundant life feels like, much less how to get it.

Discipline and conforming to the image of God's Son

A big part of what's going on is we only view life by what we see in the physical realm. But most of God's creation, and many of the things that directly impact our lives, are in the spiritual realm.

There are things going on in the spirit realm that we've never given any thought to. There are things God created and put in place to guide and train us. Yet, most of us have no awareness of them.

To show you what I mean, let's first look in Hebrews...

Hebrews 12:4-6 — "In your struggle against sin... do not make light of the Lord's discipline, and do not lose heart when he rebukes you. Because <u>the Lord disciplines the one he loves</u>, and he chastens everyone he accepts as his son." (ESV, emphasis added)

What does this say the Lord does with those he loves?

He disciplines them!

If you are a child of God, he promises to discipline you. It's not that he *might* discipline you; he *will* discipline you. It's a promise. And just as a parent disciplines a child to correct his ways and train him, our heavenly Father does the same with us.

While on this topic, it's also important to recognize that *discipline* and *punishment* are different. Discipline is for correction; punishment is for penalty. Discipline restores a person; punishment casts the person away. They feel similar because they both cause suffering. But it's the *purpose* of the suffering that differentiates the two.

God doesn't *punish* his children, but he *does* discipline them. What this means is, even if you are living what you consider a "righteous" life, God will *still* discipline you when you need to be corrected.

It's the same as we do with our children. We set rules to guide and train them. If they break the rules, we discipline them. The purpose of the discipline isn't to *punish* them... it's to *correct* them so they do it right.

That's what God does with us.

God sets the rules to guide and train us. When we break the rules, it's called "sin." And when we sin, he disciplines us to correct us, training us to do right and conforming us into the image of his Son.

That's the key... conforming to the image of his Son. But what does that really mean?

In a simplistic sense, to be "conformed to the image of his Son" means to sin *less* than we sin now and, ultimately (though not humanly possible), to become sinless — without sin, just as the Son is.

What sets us apart from the Son is sin. We have sin, the Son does not. If we could become sinless, we would be conformed to the image of God's Son.

In practical terms, learning to sin *less* means learning to live our lives not doing the things our flesh wants us to do (being "led by the flesh"), but doing the things the Lord wants us to do (being "led by the Spirit"). And even though Jesus was fully God, he was also fully Man and modeled for us how we should live. He modeled being led by the Spirit when he said in **John 5:19,** "Truly, truly, I say to you, the Son can do nothing of his own accord, but only what he sees the Father doing. For whatever the Father does, that the Son does likewise." (ESV)

In other words, Jesus conformed to the image of his Father by denying himself and only doing what the Father directed. And we, too, can conform to the image of his Son by denying ourselves and only doing what the Lord directs. The more we do that, the more conformed to his image we become.

This is where God's discipline comes in.

When we sin, we are not conforming to the image of his Son. So, God disciplines us to bring correction into our lives to help us stop that sin. When we stop it, we're conforming more towards the image of his Son.

Why does God want us to conform to his Son's image? Because anything that doesn't conform to the image of God is sin; and sin is what separates us from God. That's why he allows discipline in our lives — to train and conform us back into his image; the way he originally created Man.

Discipline originates in the spiritual realm, *even* for those who live righteously

What most people don't understand is the Lord's discipline originates in the spiritual realm, but manifests in the earthly realm as issues in our lives.

How do I know? Because when people *repent* of past sins, I've seen those issues disappear!

And this is true not only for those who live "sinful" lives, but also for those who live righteously as well.

For example, take my friend, Nick, who loves the Lord. He was a successful business owner for many years. Then, the Lord directed him to leave his business and go into full-time ministry, so he did.

That was about twenty years ago.

Today, he's an evangelist who has led hundreds of people to Christ. He is the pastor of a small church in his town. And he has such a heart for the poor that he has personally adopted more than five orphans into his home.

He reached out to me one day because he had been in pain for several years, and it had finally become unbearable. He had excruciating chest and back pain. They were so bad he couldn't even bend over or lift as little as twenty pounds (10kg). The regular medical personnel couldn't figure out what the problem was, so he felt he needed to see a specialist.

I've learned that many things like this have a spiritual root — even from sins committed *many* years earlier — so I told Nick the first thing he ought to do was the Prayer of Freedom. So, following the same process I'll show you later, he made a list of sins from his past, then prayed through the Prayer of Freedom and repented of them.

After *three days* he said, "**All of my pain is gone!**

23

Both my chest and back pains are *completely* gone, and I can bend over again!" He couldn't believe it!

What this shows is we can't always look at our circumstances with "earthly glasses" to understand what's going on. Sometimes, our issues may be due to discipline rather than natural causes.

And if those issues are tied to discipline, then to understand that discipline and learn how to get free from it, you must put on "spiritual glasses."

But before we put on those "spiritual glasses," let me share two things about this book that may be helpful to know.

The first thing is this book has two sections. **Section 1** is "What's Going On?" That's where we are now. In this section you'll learn what's going on, why it happens, and God's breakthrough plan to set you free. **Section 2** is "The Prayer." That's where you'll find the actual prayer process that sets you free.

Section 1 is a relatively short read for the average reader. Not only will it help the prayer make more sense but, most importantly, it will help you live in freedom much longer. Why? Because you'll know what's going on and how to keep from falling back into the issues you currently have.

Unfortunately, though, statistics show most readers never finish the books they start. And the *most* important part of this book is the prayer. So, even though Section 1 is important, if you rarely finish books you start or you need to urgently get rid of issues in your life, consider jumping ahead to Section 2 and start with the prayer *first*. It will work whether you understand why it works on or not.

The second thing is many people want to share this book once they start reading it. If you'd like to do the same, the easiest way to share it is to share the link you'll find at the top of each page: www.**ThePrayerOf-Freedom*Book*.com**. This redirects people directly to Amazon or other locations to read a short description about the book and get it if they desire.

So, with that said, if you're ready to keep learning what's going on, let's go to Chapter 2 and put on our "spiritual glasses" to see the Lord's discipline!

Chapter 2

'Spiritual glasses' to see the Lord's discipline

Dennis is an elderly man I've known for years. While visiting around the kitchen table one day, our conversation shifted to his adult son, Scott. For fifteen years, Scott and his family had been living in Dennis' house, unable to afford a home of their own.

Scott's career had started off strong in his mid-twenties, earning a multiple, six-figure income. But then, outside of his control, he was forced to change jobs and joined a large corporation. A year later, he was fired due to internal politics; and from that point forward, Scott never recovered financially.

After years of trying to get back on his feet, he and his family eventually had to sell their home and move across the country to live with Scott's parents. During the next fifteen years, he still couldn't "get ahead" financially. And even though he had faithfully followed the Lord for over twenty five years, something kept blocking him, and he was consistently paid well below his skill level. These years were so difficult he began to feel like life had passed him by. And he *still* couldn't afford to move out of his parents' home.

So, back to the kitchen table…

As Dennis and I talked about these things, I suggested he pray the Prayer of Freedom on Scott's behalf. And as I mentioned earlier, all the prayer really is (you'll see it in Section 2 of this book), is repenting of sins, and asking God to remove any discipline tied to them.

Dennis wasn't sure how to do it, so I led him through it word for word, right there at the kitchen table. The sight was precious — an elderly father, lovingly praying on behalf of his adult son. The entire prayer lasted ten minutes. And then, cataclysmic shifts began happening in Scott's life.

Within three weeks, Scott got an unexpectedly large pay raise at work which just about doubled his salary!

Three weeks after that, because of his increased income, he and his wife bought a new home. They could *finally* begin moving out of his parents' house.

Several months after that, Scott began getting all kinds of recognition at his job. So much so that he was asked to speak at national and international events to share what he was doing to consistently achieve such strong results.

Everything changed. It changed immediately. And what happened to change it was an elderly father praying the Prayer of Freedom on behalf of his adult son!

(Note: because of spiritual laws of authority, a parent has authority to intercede and repent on behalf of a child and help set them free, even an adult child. I'll discuss more about that in Chapter 14.)

I share this story because so many people live lives of "failure" and think, "That's just the way it is — I got dealt a bad hand." But, depending on the root of the issues, there *can* be breakthrough from failure. All it takes is knowing where to look...

"Spiritual glasses" to look into the spiritual realm

In the last chapter, I explained how the Lord's discipline comes from the spiritual realm. Now, let me take you on a short journey through the ways he disciplines us and what it looks like.

What I've come to realize over the years is the spiritual "warfare" most of us go through is actually a large part of how God disciplines and trains us. So, using that frame of reference, let's take a quick peek at what God tells us about spiritual warfare.

Ephesians 6:12 — "For we are not fighting against people made of flesh and blood, but against <u>persons without bodies</u>..." (TLB, emphasis added)

That's what our spiritual warfare is all about — it's fighting against persons without bodies.

With that said, imagine I gave you a special pair of glasses that let you see into the spiritual realm. If you put them on in a room with other people, you'd see other *persons* in the room around them (and you). They wouldn't have physical bodies though, because they are spirits that exist in the spirit realm, not the earthly realm. But they are *persons*, nonetheless.

This is the reality of the world we live in — we see people with physical bodies in the earthly realm, but there are other persons with us in the spiritual realm as well.

Now, before you get freaked out about this, let me encourage you, it's nothing to be afraid of. For example, one of the spirits you'd see is one you probably already know — the Holy Spirit. This is God's Spirit, and he is a real *person* (he's one of the three persons of the Trinity). He just doesn't have a physical body.

But that's not the only person you'd see. You'd also

see angels. Angels are spirits who operate all around us in the spiritual realm. And they are all *persons* — they all have their own thinking, their own will, and their own personality. They're aware of what's going on. The only difference is they are in a different realm than we are. They have a body in the spiritual realm, but not a body of flesh and blood like we have in the earthly realm. Make no mistake about it though… they are still "persons."

If you continue to look around with your spiritual glasses on, you're likely to see other spirits as well. For example, just a few of the spirits the Bible mentions are the spirit of wisdom, the spirit of truth, the spirit of gentleness, and even a spirit of skill (**Exodus 28:3**).

And because all of these spirits are "good" spirits, we can call them *holy* spirits — they tend to be present when people operate in holiness and righteousness.

However, as you continue looking around the room, you might also see other spirits — spirits we could call *unholy* spirits. These are spirits the Bible mentions that tend to be present when people live unholy and unrighteous lives.

For example, you might see a spirit of fear around someone, maybe a spirit of lying or anger around another, and possibly even a spirit of jealousy around others. These are all spirits of emotions; and in this case, *unholy* emotions.

Other unholy spirits you might see would be spirits of infirmity. Infirmity is anything you would go to the doctor for (i.e. your leg hurts, or you have migraines, or depression, or even things like hearing "voices" in your head). The bottom line is, if you suffer with anything that would not be considered perfect health, either mentally or physically, there may be a spirit of infirmity involved.

In fact, the Bible mentions quite a few spirits of

infirmity; among them are a spirit of fever, deafness, muteness (unable to speak), blindness, lameness (unable to walk), kyphosis (hunching of one's back), and even a spirit of seizures.

These all fall into the category of infirmities, and many times, they may be caused by spirits — by "persons without bodies" in the spiritual realm. I know it sounds a little spooky, but it's true. And it's all in the Bible.

As I've taught this throughout the years, one of the biggest push-backs I get — even from some pastors — is they have never seen the Bible reference a spirit of infirmity. So, let me show you just two examples.

The first is when Jesus heals Peter's mother-in-law who was suffering from a spirit of infirmity in the form of a fever. Here's what Luke says...

Luke 4:38-39 — "Jesus left the synagogue and went to the home of Simon. Now Simon's mother-in-law was suffering from a high fever, and they asked Jesus to help her. So he bent over her and <u>rebuked</u> the fever." (NIV, emphasis added)

Think about this for a minute. Assume I'm teaching a class, trying to write something on a whiteboard, and my marker stops working. So, what do I do? I look at the marker and say, "I rebuke you, marker!" Wouldn't that be silly?

Of course it would. Why?

Because you can't rebuke an inanimate object. You can only rebuke something that is living, something that can think and respond.

On the other hand, if someone was disrupting the class, I could rebuke the unruly student and tell him to be quiet. That would make more sense, wouldn't it?

Yes, of course. And why? Because I'd be rebuking a *person* who was doing something wrong; and that person has the ability to think and respond.

So, back to our verse above...

How can Jesus rebuke a fever?

He can only do it if it were a living thing that could think and respond — a person.

In fact, the Greek word translated as "rebuke" is epitimaō, meaning "to charge, to find fault with, or to rebuke" a person. It occurs twenty-nine times in the New Testament, and with the exception of this passage and three others, each time it is used it is clearly directed to a person (either human or spirit).

That seems to be why it is used here. This particular fever was a person — a "person without a body." It was a spirit of infirmity.

And notice what happened. As soon as Jesus rebuked it, it obeyed and left!

In another example, Jesus is teaching in a synagogue when a woman comes in who had been hunched over, unable to straighten up, for eighteen years. It was a spirit of infirmity. How do we know? Because Scripture tells us. Let's read it now...

Luke 13:10-13 — "On a Sabbath Jesus was teaching in one of the synagogues, and a woman was there who had been <u>crippled by a spirit</u> for eighteen years. She was bent over and could not straighten up at all. When Jesus saw her, he called her forward and said to her, 'Woman, you are <u>set free from your infirmity</u>.' Then he put his hands on her, and immediately she straightened up and praised God." (NIV, emphasis added)

When Luke says she was "crippled by a spirit," that means it was a spirit of infirmity that had been tormenting (crippling) the woman for eighteen years. And how did she get healed? Jesus declared she was set free, and the spirit left.

And here's the interesting thing — while it really doesn't sound like they *could* be, these spirits of infirmity are *also* part of God's creation — he created them. In fact, God created everything that exists; which means he created all spirits — both *holy* and *unholy* ones. They are all "persons without bodies," and they are all part of the goodness he put in place for us. Some protect us, some train us, and others discipline us. They all play a role in raising us up as God's children, helping us learn how to conform to the image of his Son. They are all part of his master plan.

"Spirits of Discipline"

Regardless of the specific actions each spirit does, generally speaking it's the unholy spirits God uses to discipline us. I call them "spirits of discipline" because that is their ultimate role in God's creation — to bring discipline and correction into our lives when we sin.

In other words, it's the spirits of discipline God uses to help train us in righteousness. The purpose of this discipline is to bring us to repentance and conform us to the image of his Son. That is God's ultimate goal (**Romans 8:28**), and everything he guides us through in life is focused on that singular purpose.

How do you become conformed to God's image? You must stop sinning. And the key to stop sinning is... are you ready for this? ... to *stop* doing those sinful activities!

It's like the child who gets spanked because he disobeyed his father. After being spanked for the same disobedience again and again, he eventually learns to stop doing it, and he no longer gets spanked for it.

With us, God uses spirits of discipline to bring us to repentance when *we* sin. And when we repent and stop doing those things, we stop being disciplined for them.

But here's the key — even though we may be living righteously *today*, spirits of discipline could be causing problems in our lives from sin issues committed years ago. In other words, simply because those sins have stopped and we have been living righteously ever since doesn't mean the discipline has stopped. The discipline only stops when we *repent* of those sins.

That means if you suffer with chronic health or other problems, then even if you've been living right-eously for years, those problems *could* be tied to those sins from years back... even from early childhood.

Spirits of discipline and tow truck drivers

When I was teaching on this topic before, a lady asked, "Help me understand how a loving God would send a spirit of discipline to bring all kinds of sickness or misery to someone? That just doesn't seem like the God I know and love."

And in case you're thinking the same thing, let me clarify what's going on. God is not *sending* a spirit of discipline upon anyone. However, the spiritual laws he created allow for it to happen *automatically*.

Here's an easy way to understand how it works...

Imagine a restaurant in a prime location — a uni-versity town, directly across the street from the main campus and surrounded by a bunch of dormitories. If you know anything about university towns, there's *al-ways* a shortage of parking spaces. And with the restau-rant in such a prime location, it would be tempting for students to park there and go to class or visit their friends in the dorms. But the restaurant owner doesn't want that to happen — it would block space for his cus-tomers to park and he could lose business.

So, how does the restaurant owner solve this prob-lem?

First, he makes an agreement with a towing company that gives them the legal right to tow any car in his parking lot that is not a customer. Then, he posts signs that read, "*For restaurant customers only! All unauthorized vehicles will be towed!*" You've seen those signs before, right?

What happens next is this...

The towing company sends out trucks driven by guys whose only job is to look for illegally parked cars. They get paid for every car they find and tow away. So, they are motivated to look everywhere, all the time, hoping to find the next violator. And as soon as they find a violator, they have a legal right to tow the car and charge what the student claims is an exorbitant fee to get his car back.

Now that you've got the scenario, here's one way it could play out in real life...

Jim needs to give some papers to a friend who's studying on campus. It's late at night, the restaurant is closed, the parking lot is empty, and the building where his friend is studying is just a few minutes' walk from the parking lot. So, Jim swings into the parking lot, walks across the street to drop off the papers, and returns. The entire process takes less than fifteen minutes, but by the time he returns, his car is gone! The guy in the tow truck already took it away!

Jim is obviously upset. After all, he was only there fifteen minutes. Not only that, but the parking lot was *empty* — the restaurant wasn't even using it at that moment, so it wasn't hurting anyone else for him to park there. The towing company took his car and is now going to *steal* (in his opinion) his money if he wants to get it back. It doesn't seem fair.

Who can Jim complain to?

It wasn't the restaurant owner's fault. In fact, the owner never *sent* the tow truck to take Jim's car away.

So Jim can't complain to the owner.

Additionally, it wasn't the towing company's fault. The tow company had a legal right to remove any violator who parked there illegally, regardless of what time it was.

It was Jim's fault! He saw the signs, he knew the risks involved. But he thought it wasn't a big deal — he thought he could "get away with it."

And that, in a sense, is how the process works with spirits of discipline. It's a legal structure with rules that are set up and authorized by God, and the whole thing operates automatically. The rules and consequences are posted. And certain spirits are "hovering" around, constantly looking for violators. As soon as you break the rules, they now have a legal right to bring discipline into your life.

How, *specifically*, do these spirits of discipline work?

That's what we'll cover in the next chapter.

Chapter 3

How spirits of discipline work

Thirteen-year-old Riley asked, "Is it normal to feel physically *lighter* after doing this?" as she giddily danced around the kitchen.

I had known Riley and her family for over ten years, and in the past six years I had never seen Riley smile, let alone *dance* for joy. Now, she was skipping about the house, humming to herself, and had the biggest smile you could imagine!

Beaming from ear to ear at what the Lord had just done in her life, I answered, "Yes, it is. That's what freedom feels like."

Fifteen minutes earlier, she was a different person. So different that you wouldn't even believe this was the same girl. For the last number of years, she had always been sullen and morose. She was dark — in her appearance, the way she dressed, her personality, her outlook on life. But something changed when I led her through the simple Prayer of Freedom.

I was at her home because, a few days earlier, her mom served divorce papers against her dad. Her life was crumbling around her, and I was there to help pray them through these issues.

When I first spoke with Riley that day, I asked, "Riley, do you ever feel like you're carrying a heavy load around all the time, like a great, big backpack filled with rocks?"

From her hunched over position, I could barely

make out her mumbled reply, "Yes. It feels like a _heavy_ backpack."

I went on to ask, "Do you feel darkness in your life?"

"All the time!" came her immediate response as she looked up at me. I had obviously struck a nerve.

"Do you feel depressed?" "Yes," she said.

That's when I guided her through the Prayer of Freedom. And after she prayed, it was all gone! All the darkness, all the heaviness weighing her down... everything.

Now, you may not be a thirteen-year-old girl, but I bet you can relate to what Riley was going through. If I asked those same questions of you, how would _you_ answer?

Do you feel like you're carrying around a heavy backpack that seems to get heavier each day? Is your life dark? Are you burdened with depression or anxiety?

If yes, the Prayer of Freedom can help _you_ get free from it all, too.

And, if you are a parent of young children, I've seen the Prayer of Freedom calm all types of behavior issues, as well. And it calms them _immediately_. I'll share more about that in Section 2.

God and Michelangelo — how God conforms us to his image

An easy way to understand how God conforms us to his image is to think of a sculptor carving a beautiful, marble statue.

For example, one of the most famous statues in the world is "David" by Michelangelo. When people would ask Michelangelo how he created such a beautiful masterpiece from a block of stone, his simple reply was: "I saw the person inside the stone, and carved away everything that wasn't part of him until I set him free."

Michelangelo was a master sculptor, and he used a number of tools, each with a specific purpose. When just getting started, he used large, "heavy chipping" chisels and hammers to chip away large pieces of stone. The goal was to get down to the person locked inside the block as quickly as possible. Next, as he got closer to the "person," he'd change to smaller, "detail sculpting" chisels. These allowed him to chip away smaller pieces of stone, working free the finer details of his masterpiece. Finally, when he had fully "freed" the person from the block of stone, he would then use a range of polishing cloths — similar to sandpaper — to smooth out the rough, chipped edges, making it as smooth as skin.

And, in a sense, God does the same with us.

The focus of discipline is to chip away everything that doesn't conform to his image.

In the beginning when God created Man, Man was made in God's image. But when sin entered the picture, we lost that image. Since then, sin has continued to cling to humanity and formed a block of "stone" all around us. So, by the time we were born, we were already encased in a block of sin and unrecognizable as God's children.

And just as Michelangelo did, God uses different tools to remove the block of sin from around us. While Michelangelo used metal chisels, God uses spirits of discipline. Some are aggressive and chip away large chunks of sin quickly. Others are more detail-focused, chipping away tiny, individual sins in our lives until they are removed. Finally, once we are fully freed, he uses finer, polishing tools that smooth off the remaining rough edges of sin that still cling to our lives.

Spirits of discipline and repentance

That's the purpose of the spirits of discipline — to free us from the sin that blocks us from the image of God.

The Biblical term for this is repentance. When you break the rules, it's called "sin." When you acknowledge you were wrong and turn the other direction, it's called "repentance." That's the goal of discipline, to bring about repentance.

When we sin against God, it's the spirits of discipline that help guide us to repentance so we can be conformed back to God's image. This is how God's process works.

We see the beginning stages of this in the New Testament with John the Baptist. Do you remember what his primary message was?

It was, "Repent!"

Do you remember the principal message Jesus came to preach?

It was the same message — "Repent! For the kingdom of heaven is in your midst." Everything else Jesus taught falls under the umbrella of "repent!"

And why is repentance so important that it was both John the Baptist's and Jesus' main message?

Because repentance is the key to conforming back to the image of God!

The two consequences of sin

To understand why repentance is so important, you first have to understand what sin does. And in very simple terms, sin does two things.

First, sin breaks our relationship with God.

Man was created to have fellowship with God. And as long as Man (Adam) remained without sin, that relationship was intact. However, as soon as Adam sinned, the relationship was broken... and it's been broken ever since.

Second, sin breaks our image of God.

Man was created in the image of God. That image was a perfect, righteous, sinless image. But when Adam sinned, it broke his image of God, and all future generations have been made in *Adam's* image, not God's image (**Genesis 5:3**). Our image of God has been broken ever since.

Later (about 2,000 years ago), God sent his Son, Jesus, to live a perfect, sinless life and die on the cross as a sacrifice for us to restore all that was lost through sin — both our relationship with God and our image of God.

So, how do we restore our *relationship* with God?

We repent of our sins *as a whole* and believe in Jesus' death on the cross to have freed us from those sins. By faith, believing in Jesus and repenting of our sins, our relationship is restored with Father God.

But what about God's image — how do we restore the *image* of God?

It's similar, but slightly different. We repent of our sins, but instead of repenting of them as a whole we must repent of them *individually* — repent for each sin.

Since each individual sin breaks a portion of God's image from us, we must repent of each sin individually to restore that portion of God's image back to us. This is how God's discipline works — he disciplines us for *each* unrepented sin, individually. So, to be released from the discipline, we must, therefore, repent of each sin individually.

I know that may sound hard to do this — to try and remember sins you've committed over the years so you can repent of them — but the process that is built into the Prayer of Freedom makes it very easy. I'll share more on that in Section 2 of this book.

Now that we've got a glimpse of the process and what spirits of discipline are for, let's look at *how* they do it in our lives. To do that, we'll need to go back in time to the Middle Ages...

Chapter 4

Parable of the Unmerciful Servant

Medieval England, Circa 1450 A.D.

The frightened prisoners cringed as another eerie scream of agony filled the barely lit dungeon halls.

"AAAHHHH!!!"

They were all well aware that the tormented cries were coming from the lower depths.

"AAAHHHH!!!"

That's where "the device" was kept. A sadistic new invention created by a truly demented man with only one goal in mind. To inflict pain!

"AAAHHHH!!!"

There were whispers throughout the land that it was a giant wheel with a geared crank on it. First, the offender's hands were tied to the wheel and his feet were tied to the wall. Then, the jailer would slowly crank the gears of the giant wheel. Each incremental turn of the wheel would slowly pull the prisoner's limbs apart, bit by bit, until they ripped out of their sockets.

CRACK...

POP...

"AAAHHHH!!!"

Some people called it "the rack," but no matter its

name, everyone knew there was no one who could withstand its gruesome torture. If they wanted a confession out of you, they would get it... *in turn*.

The Parable of the Unmerciful Servant

A somewhat disturbing image, isn't it?

But what does it have to do with God and spirits of discipline? More than you might imagine! Let me explain...

In Matthew 18, Jesus shares a parable called the Parable of the Unmerciful Servant. Let's take a look at it.

Matthew 18:21 (NIV) — "Then Peter came to Jesus and asked, 'Lord, how many times shall I forgive my brother or sister who sins against me? Up to seven times?'"

I want to set up this scenario for you here. As he usually does, Peter thinks he's going above and beyond what he should be doing here — "As many as *seven* times?! This is great. That's gotta be a lot, right?"

But Jesus, as he does so many times (with all of us), puts Peter back in his place. Here's what he says:

v. 22 — "Jesus answered, 'I tell you, not seven times, but seventy times seven.'"

Next, Jesus tells a story, called a parable, to articulate a spiritual truth about the kingdom of heaven. By the way, we live in the kingdom of heaven. It's not *up there*. As Jesus said earlier, "Repent, for the kingdom of heaven is in your midst." We are living *inside* the kingdom of heaven now, so what he's sharing here is what happens within this kingdom.

vv. 23-24 — "Therefore, the kingdom of heaven is like a king who wanted to settle accounts with his servants. As he began the settlement, a man who owed him ten thousand bags of gold was brought to him…"

Just to put that into perspective, that's around $18 *billion* USD today!

vv. 25-26 — "Since he was not able to pay, the master ordered that he and his wife and his children and all that he had be sold to repay the debt. At this, the servant fell on his knees before him, 'Be patient with me,' he begged, 'And I will pay back everything.'"

Do you think he could?

No way. It's too much.

vv. 27-28a — "The servant's master took pity on him, cancelled the debt, and let him go. But when that servant went out, he found one of his fellow servants who owed him one hundred silver coins…"

One hundred silver coins is about $10,000 in today's terms. This shows the magnitude of difference between the two servants' debts.

vv. 28b-34 — "He grabbed him and began to choke him, 'Pay back what you owe me!' he demanded. His fellow servant fell to his knees and begged him, 'Be patient with me, and I will pay it back.' But he refused. Instead, he went off and had the man thrown into prison until he could pay the debt. When the other servants saw what had happened, they were outraged and went and told their master everything that had happened. Then, the master called the servant in, 'You wicked servant!' he said, 'I cancelled all that debt of yours because you begged me to. Shouldn't you have had mercy on your fellow servant just as I had on you?' In anger, his master handed him over to the jailers to be tortured until he should pay back all that he owed."

Now, if you look at various translations of this passage, you'll find that some versions only use the word 'jailer' and leave out the 'tortured' part of it. But when that happens, you'll usually find a footnote that says,

"Some manuscripts also include 'to be tortured.'"

Jesus is telling a story about something important here. But what does it have to do with Peter's question regarding forgiveness? And what in the world does it have to do with spirits of discipline?

Let me see if I can paint this picture for you so we can go a little deeper…

This parable is about a country ruled by a king, and he has subjects who live in it. The king sets rules on how his kingdom should operate. If you break the rules, you are disciplined.

So, what's the role of the jailer in all of this?

It's discipline — if you break the rules, you visit the jailer. He's the one who performs the discipline.

The Greek word being translated as 'jailer' means: "a torturer; a person who extracts the truth from others through use of the rack." And the rack was a tool used to torture someone.

That's why a person was sent to the jailer, to be tortured. The jailer was an expert at it.

The image I get of this jailer is something along the lines of a filthy, ugly man with a hunched back and warts all over his face. And each time he cranks the wheel of the rack, one turn… another turn… another… he cackles with evil delight. He just loves hearing those screams of agony! Causing pain in someone's life is what he lives for.

So, think about this…

It's not likely the king and the jailer are friends. It's not likely they are in the same socio-economic circles of kingdom society.

While you have that evil, ugly jailer down in the dungeon, at the same time you have the king up in his castle. He's clean, majestic, wearing royal robes, and he loves his subjects. The two are so diametrically opposed that they don't even seem to go together.

Yet, the jailer plays a significant role in the king-dom. And the king actually *pays* the jailer to do his job of administering discipline.

No one *wants* to see the jailer, so they do good. But if they do bad, they are sent to the jailer. And when they come back out again, they don't want to do bad any-more. That makes sense, right?

With that, now we get to the main message Jesus is teaching in his parable.

Keep in mind, Jesus is not telling this parable to the Jewish leaders. He's not talking to the Pharisees, or to the people who have rejected him. He's not even talking to the crowds who come and listen to him. Jesus is talk-ing to his closest disciples. He's talking to Peter and the Twelve. And here's what he says…

v. 35 - "This is how my Heavenly Father will treat each of you, unless you forgive your brother from your heart."

Notice he doesn't say, "My Heavenly Father *might* do this." He says, "My Heavenly Father *will* do this."

What Jesus is talking about is *discipline* — in this case, for unforgiveness. Unforgiveness is a sin. And be-cause all sins are similar — they all break the image of God — they all have the same process of correction.

That correction is discipline. But discipline comes in different forms. Just as with children — sometimes a child gets spanked; at other times he goes to time-out; and other times he loses privileges. Regardless of the form, it's all discipline to bring about correction.

It's the same way with God. His discipline may take different forms for each person and for each sin, but it's all discipline, nonetheless. That's what Jesus is convey-ing to us.

But how does our Heavenly Father discipline us?

Well, a little sleuthing around in the world of Greek translations will reveal a scary truth.

When you look at the word translated as "jailer," the root of that word comes from a Greek word called *basanizo*. And it's this *basanizo* that is the form through which much of God's discipline comes to us.

Let's look at it now — it *will* surprise you!

Chapter 5

Three forms of *"basanizo"* discipline

My wife and I are friends with a single mom named Jan. She has two young children and has recently been going through nasty legal problems with her ex-husband.

He had been criminally accused for things related to why the divorce happened, and whenever he spends time with the kids, the court requires him to be supervised for the children's safety. Even so, every time the kids are with him, they're terrified. Just the mention that they are going to spend time with their father scares them.

Despite the charges against him, the ex-husband was still trying to gain custody of the kids and do all he could to reduce his child support.

For months, neither of the children would talk about their fear; and whenever Jan asked, they would just close up. But she kept praying that their "voices" would be heard so the court could better understand the situation and protect them.

When Jan shared this, I just felt in my heart like it was a spiritual battle more than anything else. Knowing a few things regarding the husband's background, I thought it might be something coming down through his family line, or possibly even Jan's (I'll explain more about this in a later chapter). That's when I suggested Jan pray the Prayer of Freedom.

And she did.

About two or three days later she told me, "I prayed that prayer you sent me, and there was a *significant* breakthrough with the children. Both of them, individually, started opening up to me on their own about their dad. They started talking and sharing their feelings about how he scares them. And it wasn't just a short conversation either — it was a *flood* of conversation. Each one just kept talking and talking, as if their voices had been dammed up for a long time, and the dam finally burst, letting it all come out!"

It was such a breakthrough for Jan that she was almost in tears.

If you've never been in a similar situation, it may not seem like a big deal to you. But for Jan, who was at her wits end on how to get the children to open up so the judge could hear their voices, it was *huge*!

And it was, in some mysterious way, a spirit of discipline that was holding them back.

Spirits of discipline operate in various ways. For Jan, they were blocking the children's voices from being heard. For others, it's something else.

Let's look now at three of the most common ways these spirits operate...

Basanizo discipline

As I mentioned in the last chapter, the root word in the Greek for 'jailer' is *basanizo*. This word means: "to torture, to inflict pain, to torment."

Basanizo is the process through which much of God's discipline takes place in our lives. This word is used only twelve times in the New Testament, but I want to walk you through just three of those passages to show you some of the different forms discipline can take in our lives.

I believe it will help because once you recognize it, you will no longer look with earthly eyes at your earthly circumstances and say, "These issues I'm going through are simply due to natural causes," or "I have no idea why I'm going through these things." Instead, once you understand what you're looking for, you can say, "This feels like a spirit of discipline in my life. Let me think through what I might have done that I would be disciplined for." Then, with the Prayer of Freedom, you'll be able to stop it.

So, are you ready to see what *basanizo* does in our lives?

Alright, let's look...

▸ *Basanizo* Discipline #1 - physical suffering

The first passage is found in Matthew 8 with the story of the centurion and his sick servant.

Matthew 8:5-6 — "When he had entered Capernaum, a centurion came forward to him, appealing to him, 'Lord, my servant is lying paralyzed at home, suffering terribly.'" (ESV)

"Suffering" is the word *basanizo*. And what was he suffering from?

Paralysis.

Physical suffering is one form of *basanizo* discipline — it can manifest in any part of your body as something that isn't functioning properly.

I remember one day, my wife and I were at Wal-Mart. We saw a young, homeless couple named Nita and Brad outside the entrance, so we asked if we could pray for them. In the conversation, they mentioned they had just been given an apartment, so we took them inside to buy a few things to help them set up their new home.

While we were there, I picked up a book on spiritual growth for them. And as we were walking down the aisle, I was teasing Brad, saying, "You'll have to fight Nita for the book if you want to read it."

But Nita said, "Oh no, Brad will read it to me because I can't read."

I went, "Aww, I'm sorry. I didn't know you couldn't read. What happened... have you never learned?"

And she said, "Oh, no, it's not that. I know how to read, but I just can't see to read. Everything is blurry."

At that point, Nita was standing several feet from Brad. This was during wintertime, and Brad had on a knit ski cap with great big, two-inch tall letters on it that read, "LEVI'S." I asked, "Can you read the word "LEVI'S" on his hat?"

She said, "No, they are too blurry."

So I said, "Well, I don't think the Lord wants you to have blurry vision. Let's pray for it."

I then led her through a short version of the Prayer of Freedom. And in asking her questions about things that might be unrepented sins, I asked if she had unforgiveness in her heart for anyone.

She admitted, "Yes, my ex-boyfriend. He grabbed me by the back of my head and slammed my face into the dresser over and over again, breaking out all my teeth, top and bottom." To verify this, she showed me she had no teeth in the front of her mouth.

I asked if she would be willing to forgive him, and she said yes. So I led her in a short prayer of forgiveness. Then, I asked the Lord to open her eyes so she could see clearly.

To test it out, I asked her again if she could read the word "LEVI'S" on Brad's hat, and this time, she could! I then opened the book we got for them, held it about four feet away, and asked if she could read it, too!

... And she DID! She began reading the book from four feet away. The Lord perfectly restored her vision!

Her blurry eyesight was due to a spirit of discipline. It was a physical suffering that impacted her eyes.

That's one form of *basanizo*.

▶ *Basanizo* Discipline #2 - mental suffering

The second passage we'll look at is in 2 Peter, where he is talking about sin, fallen angels, and the like. We'll pick up the passage here...

2 Peter 2:7-8 — "And if he rescued righteous Lot, greatly distressed by the sensual conduct of the wicked (for as that righteous man lived among them day after day, he was <u>tormenting</u> his righteous soul over their lawless deeds that he saw and heard)." (ESV)

"Tormenting" is the Greek word *basanizo*. And in this case, it's used to describe **mental suffering**. Mental suffering can be anything from depression, darkness, heaviness, anxiety, stress, and much more.

How does this play out with us today?

I remember a story from a pastor named Richard. His son, Andy, was a youth pastor. Andy went through a really nasty divorce that his wife initiated. It was terrible. It tore Andy up, and he went spiraling downward. He was in such a state of depression that he lost his job and wouldn't even leave the house for *two* years.

For those two years, his pastor-dad was on his knees every day battling for his son in prayer, but nothing ever changed.

Then, one day the Lord opened Richard's eyes to understand more about the foundational truths behind the Prayer of Freedom. The Lord told Richard to repent on behalf of his son. So Richard repented for all the sins he imagined Andy had probably been dealing with — anger, frustration, hurt, unforgiveness, all these things. The entire prayer session lasted about fifteen minutes. That's it.

About ten days later, Andy calls up Richard and says, "Dad, you won't believe what happened. Ten days ago, the depression instantly left! I feel totally normal now!"

It was a spirit of discipline — mental suffering in the form of depression. And it lasted until those sins were repented of. And an interesting thing about this case is it was his *father* who repented for his sins, not himself (just like what happened with the elderly father in Chapter 2 who repented on behalf of *his* son).

▶ *Basanizo* Discipline #3 - physical pain

The last example of *basanizo* I want to share is from Revelation. And this shows yet another form it can take in our lives.

Revelation 12:2 — "She was pregnant and was crying out in birth pains and the <u>agony</u> of giving birth." (ESV)

"Agony" is the Greek word *basanizo*. And in this instance, *basanizo* shows up as **physical pain**.

Another experience I had with *basanizo* discipline was at the drug addiction recovery center where I teach as a volunteer. Word had spread about my praying for people, and a woman named Susan came up and asked if I would pray for her.

I said "Sure, what's wrong?"

She said, "I've had rheumatoid arthritis for fifteen or twenty years, and it's *really* been flaring up these last several days."

So, I began going through the Prayer of Freedom with her; and as I did, I asked, "Do you have unforgiveness for anyone?"

She said, "Yes."

"Would you be willing to forgive them?"

Again, she said, "Yes."

I led her in a condensed version of the Prayer of Freedom, "Lord, I forgive so and so..." After that, I asked the Lord to take away her arthritis pain. Then, I asked her to test it out.

She went up and down a flight of stairs, and when she came back, she exclaimed, "It feels a *lot* better!"

After I left, I didn't give it much thought until a few weeks later. I had just finished teaching a class when Susan walks in. She tracked me down because she wanted to give me an update. And this is what she said...

"Ever since you prayed for me six weeks ago, I've had *no* arthritis pain."

I said, "Praise the Lord! That's wonderful!"

She continued, "I just came back from the doctor two or three days ago. He retested me and told me that I don't have *any* arthritis in my body at all."

Again, I said, "That's wonderful!"

But then, she said one more thing that was even more amazing....

She went on, "... not only that, but the doctor said my body shows no signs of *ever* having had arthritis in the past!"

It was simply a spirit of discipline in the form of physical suffering.

This is one of the things I often see. When an infirmity is due to a spirit of discipline and you repent of the sin for which you're being disciplined, not only does the discipline stop but, frequently, God will restore the *physical* damage that the discipline created!

It's mind-boggling and exciting, don't you think?

But what does all of this mean?

What it means to me is simple…

When you go through any kind of challenge in your life — aches, pains, relationship issues, and more — it might be a spirit of discipline. And if it is, all it takes to stop the suffering is the Prayer of Freedom!

But isn't suffering supposed to be "good" for us?

I grew up in a church that preached that "suffering is good for us" because God uses it to help us grow and mature. And, to a certain degree, they're right.

So, the question comes up, "if suffering is good for me, should I attempt to *stop* it?"

That's actually a very good question. Sometimes, the suffering we go through *should* be stopped. But other times, it shouldn't.

If you've been taught that suffering is good, as I had, here's a simple explanation to make sense of it all…

When the Bible teaches about suffering, it teaches primarily about two types. One is for disobeying God; the other is for obeying him.

▸ Suffering for disobeying God

When we sin and disobey God, God disciplines us, causing us to suffer. This is where spirits of discipline come in. The purpose of discipline (and its suffering) is to bring about correction. That correction happens when we repent.

So, when we suffer because we disobey God, the suffering is "good" because it causes us to repent and turn from those sins.

▸ Suffering for obeying God

The other type of suffering is when we obey God and do what he has called us to do. When we do, Jesus *promises* we will be persecuted. And that persecution brings about suffering.

Suffering from persecution feels similar to that of discipline except, rather than suffering because you are disobeying God, you're now suffering because you are *obeying* him. You're doing what he has called you to do, and the enemy is trying to stop you from doing it.

This suffering is also good, but in a different way. While suffering from discipline is good for bringing about correction, suffering from persecution is good because it's the type of suffering Jesus went through. And God honors us when we obey him to the point that others persecute us for the sake of his name.

So, what can we conclude from all of this?

If your suffering is because of *disobedience* — you have sinned and God is disciplining you — then yes... it *is* good to repent of your sin and stop the suffering.

If your suffering is because of *obedience* — you are obeying God and the enemy is trying to stop you — then no... it is *not* good to stop the suffering. To stop the suffering of persecution means you must stop doing what the Lord has called you to do.

With that said, there is one more thing you need to understand to get rid of your suffering due to sin and discipline. It's called "legal rights." Understanding legal rights is the key to being set free.

I'll share more about this in the next chapter. However, if you're eager to start praying and get free *now*, you can jump ahead to Section 2 and begin the prayer section, then afterwards return to this page and continue on from here.

Chapter 6

Legal Rights

Before I get into explaining legal rights, I first have a pop quiz for you…

Oh no! I bet you weren't expecting this!

I assure you; you'll probably pass it easily enough. All you have to do is recognize the type of discipline involved with the following story. Here it is…

A friend of mine, Bill, is in his early 50's. About thirty-five years ago he broke his right hip playing college football and has been in pain ever since. The pain had been getting progressively worse over the years. Anytime he walked, the pain was excruciating! By the time I spoke with him a few months ago (as of the time I'm writing this), it had become so severe that he had been walking with a cane for over a year.

In fact, it was so bad that the doctors had been telling him for the last several years he needed full hip replacement surgery.

So, what was this 'excruciating pain' he was experiencing?

Correct! It ended up being *discipline* in the form of 'physical pain.'

And what did Bill need to do to get rid of it?

That's right — he needed to *repent* of whatever sin was the root cause of the issue.

So, I stepped in to help him find out what it was…

As he was sharing about his hip, my heart felt like this was probably a *basanizo*-type discipline rather than just natural causes, so I began asking a few questions. Going through the Prayer of Freedom process, I was looking for any unrepented sins he might have done before his accident.

As a side note, I don't think his football accident, by itself, was *basanizo* discipline. But I've learned that when an injury doesn't heal and only gets progressively worse, it is often *basanizo*. That's what I was probing for here.

As we talked, he shared that he was sexually active in high school. Since I couldn't find any other significant sin he had done, I felt that may have been the issue we were looking for. So, I led him in a short version of the Prayer of Freedom, had him repent of that sin, then asked the Lord to heal his hip.

What happened next was amazing!

I asked him to stand up and check it out.

He stood up and started crying. Now, Bill is a big guy, so I wasn't expecting that at all!

After about two or three minutes, he regained his composure and said, "Beatty, I'm *completely* out of pain!" He started walking around the house without his cane, and without *any* pain.

This was the first time in thirty-five years his hip had been pain free — the pain was totally gone!

But here's something worth noting…

The pain was a physical issue in which all the x-rays and tests showed the hip was worn out and needed to be fully replaced. The doctors had confirmed it multiple times. But even though there was physical damage, the ultimate root behind it was spiritual.

And that spiritual root was?

You guessed it — unrepented sin.

This is what the Parable of the Unmerciful Servant

shows us. If you sin and disobey God, and don't repent of that sin, then God will allow a spirit of discipline in your life *for your own good*. He wants to bring correction in your life and guide you to repentance. Why? Because that's the process it takes to conform you into the image of his Son. That's the whole purpose of discipline.

And as I mentioned back in the first chapter, God does this because he loves you.

God's discipline is for our good... *because* he loves us

Now, let's look at a few more scriptures that show God's ultimate purpose with all of this. The first one is from Hebrews.

Hebrews 12:7b-11 — "For what children are not disciplined by their fathers? ... We have all had human fathers who disciplined us, and we respected them for it... They disciplined us for a little while as they thought best. But God disciplines us for our good, in order that we may share in his holiness. No discipline seems pleasant at the time, but painful. Later on, however, it produces a harvest of righteousness and peace for those who have been trained by it." (NIV, emphasis added)

Notice two things about God's discipline. First, it's "for our good." And second, it brings "righteousness and peace" once you've been trained by it.

If righteousness (a life of repentance) and peace come from being trained by discipline, what happens when you have *not* been trained by it?

That's right — you live a life of unrighteousness (sin without repentance) and you lack peace.

If your life is filled with constant frustration and

turmoil — either with relationship problems, external problems beyond your control, job issues, chronic health concerns, infertility, and the like — and you have no peace in those areas, the root problem may be a lack of righteousness.

To illustrate this even more, let's look at a familiar passage in the Gospel of John. This is about the lame man at the pool. Now that you're learning more about *basanizo* discipline, this passage might make more sense to you as to what's really going on. We find it in **John 5:2-9, 14** (ESV)...

vv. 2-3 — "Now there is in Jerusalem by the Sheep Gate a pool, in Aramaic called Bethesda, which has five roofed colonnades. In these lay a multitude of invalids—blind, lame, paralyzed."

Can you see the spirit of *basanizo* in there? "Blind, lame, paralyzed."

vv. 5-9, 14a — "One man was there who had been an invalid for thirty-eight years. When Jesus saw him lying there and knew that he had already been there a long time... Jesus said to him, 'Get up, take up your bed, and walk.' And at once the man was healed, and he took up his bed and walked... Afterward, Jesus found him in the temple and said to him, 'See, you are well...'"

Now watch this. This is the part most people don't understand...

v. 14b — "Sin no more, that nothing *worse* may happen to you." (emphasis added)

It appears there was a spirit of discipline bringing *basanizo* torment in the form of paralysis and physical suffering. We infer from Jesus' final statement that this man must have done something in the past to bring this discipline on himself. Otherwise, why would Jesus tell him, "Sin no more, that nothing *worse* may happen to you?" He didn't say that to everyone he healed, but he *did* say it to this man!

Whatever the case may be, spirits of discipline are allowed by God to torment us for one reason. And that is to bring about correction in our lives due to unrepented sin. They are there to bring us to repentance of specific sins so we can be conformed to the image of Christ.

The process *always* begins with repentance. You repent first, then you get breakthrough. You repent first, then you get freedom. Every single time, it starts with repentance.

Why? Because it's turning away from the sin that holds us back from conforming to him. It's the chipping away of the stone of sin that blocks our image of Christ.

Unrepented sin and "legal rights"

Unrepented sin gives spirits of discipline a "legal right" to torment us. This is the key to understanding God's discipline and how the Prayer of Freedom works.

Remember, spirits of discipline are usually *unholy* spirits. Unholy spirits are those that oppose God. They don't like God. Yet, in some mysterious way, God created them *because* he loves us. They are one of his methods to bring us to repentance.

If you go back to the jailer in the Parable of the Unmerciful Servant, this process starts to make more sense…

The jailer hates the king. He doesn't like serving the king. But when people break the law, they go before a judge who renders a judgment and sends them to the dungeon. The judgment notice goes with the lawbreaker and is then given to the jailer. When he sees it (his legal right to torment), he gets excited and says, "Up on the rack with you — it's my turn, now!" (pun intended!)

That judgment says you are convicted of breaking the law, and it's that conviction that serves as the legal right for the jailer to do what he loves to do: to cause pain in your life.

In the spirit world, the legal right is unrepented sin. It gives these spirits of discipline a right to torment us, and when someone has unrepented sin giving them a legal right to attack, those spirits are *unable* to resist — they are wired to respond. And bringing pain, torment, and suffering is the only thing they know how to do, and they *long* to do it.

The thief that destroys

Jesus speaks about these spirits in **John 10:10** — "The thief comes only to steal, kill and destroy. I came that [you] may have life and have it abundantly." (ESV, clarification added)

The "thief" is a spirit of discipline. The "steal, kill and destroy" is the pain and suffering the spirit brings into your life. *God* doesn't bring the pain and suffering into your life — it is your sin that gives the "thief" the legal right to do it.

Do you remember the analogy I shared in Chapter 2 with the restaurant and the tow truck company, and how Jim got his car towed because he parked illegally? That's how these legal rights work. God doesn't *send* suffering into your life. But because of his spiritual laws, whenever you sin *you* create legal rights that invite spirits of discipline to bring the suffering to you.

And the only way to get the "abundant life" Jesus speaks about is to repent of the sins that give the thief a legal right to "steal, kill and destroy." Once you do, it removes the legal right, and it stops.

So, even though the unholy spirits don't want to serve the Lord, they can't avoid serving him. By doing what they are created to do, they actually do God's will — they bring us to repentance!

Anaphylactic shock disappears

A while back I had emailed the Prayer of Freedom to a friend of mine named Kate. She had been going through some issues I thought it might help her with.

But in a completely different turn of events, something else unexpected happened…

Mike, her husband, had been working out at the gym a lot and drinking protein shakes every day. He kept trying different brands to see which one he liked best.

One day, he drank a shake from a new brand — one with flax seed protein — and immediately had an allergic reaction to it. He went into anaphylactic shock, his throat started closing up, and it became difficult to breathe!

Kate was scared! She was just getting him in the car to rush him to the ER when she remembered the process of the Prayer of Freedom. So she prayed — she quickly repented for sins Mike might have committed, then asked the Lord to heal him.

Instantly, his throat opened up and he started breathing normally!

(Note: because of the marriage covenant that makes husband and wife "one," one spouse can repent on behalf of the other and help set them free. I'll share more about this in Chapter 14.)

Which sins created "legal rights" to your life?

How did Kate know which sins to repent of? My best guess is she repented of anything she could think of, and probably did a blanket prayer, "I repent for *all* of Mike's sins." But whatever she did, it worked!

Every unrepented sin creates legal rights in the spirit realm. And it's these legal rights that allow spirits of discipline to bring suffering in your life. This includes sins you know you committed, those you don't realize you committed, things you did that you may not even consider to be sinful, and sometimes even things others do to you without your consent.

This whole world of spiritual warfare is much bigger than most people realize, and has far reaching implications in the quality of life we live.

And there is both good and bad news tied to it...

The good news is you can have a life of righteousness and peace — all you have to do is choose to repent. The bad news is you can have a life of unrighteousness, torment, and darkness — all you have to do is... *not* repent.

Now, I know you're probably thinking, "But, I repented of my sins years ago when I chose to follow Jesus. I thought all my sins were forgiven — past, present, and future. So, why do I need to repent again?"

You see, unlike the general prayer of repentance for salvation — where we say something like, "Lord Jesus, I repent of my sins. I believe in you and commit my life to you," and we're born again — when it comes to God's discipline, we must repent of each sin, individually and specifically. It's only when the specific sins are repented of, individually, that you remove their legal rights for spirits of discipline to attack.

As I shared earlier — just like with the jailer and his prisoner — it's only when the legal right (the "judgment") is removed that the discipline and torment can be stopped.

A lot of times when I teach this, I look out over the crowd and see worried faces staring back at me. I'm asked, "But I've sinned soooo much in my life over the years — how in the world am I expected to remember every sin I did so I can repent of them?"

The simple answer is: it's God's responsibility to remind you of the sins that need to repented of so you can freed from your torment. Trust me... he wants you free more than *you* do!

All of this is part of the process with the Prayer of Freedom. I'll explain more in Section 2 of this book. Read on...

Chapter 7

Sin is a cause for infirmity (Old Testament)

friend of mine in Uganda, named John, emailed me a while back, asking for money to send his sister to the doctor. She had been poisoned and desperately needed to see a specialist. Another woman in their village had also been poisoned earlier on and died, so John was extremely concerned about his sister.

The Lord prompted me to first send him the Prayer of Freedom. So I did, told him to pray through it, and get back to me within three days. If there was no change, then I would send the money. Here is his email three days later, slightly adjusted for clarity and brevity...

"Greetings from Uganda,

"My sister, TJ, is a 16-year-old student studying in Level 3 of high school. As I mentioned, last month she started experiencing itching in her throat, had a terrible stomachache, and had constant headaches.

"After testing for malaria and typhoid, we took her to a medical specialist for further tests. Those tests revealed she had been poisoned! The doctor gave her an antidote, but it wasn't effective.

"By this time, TJ was unable to eat, unable to walk, bedridden, and in critical condition. It became clear she needed more intensive medical treatment. That's when I reached out to you.

"When you gave me the Prayer of Freedom, I shared it with my mother and TJ, and we all prayed it for three days as you directed us. When we did, amazing changes happened!

"TJ got her appetite back and began eating again, she was able to get out of bed and started walking again, and the stomachache completely disappeared!

"We took her back to the medical personnel for testing; and after running more tests, the doctors confirmed the poison was essentially gone! All TJ needed now was an inexpensive supplement to help a little with her kidneys.

"The power of prayer made a life-changing difference in my sister's life. Thank you for sharing the Prayer of Freedom with us."

The "miracles" of the Prayer of Freedom

On a personal note, I never cease to be amazed at the results people get with the Prayer of Freedom. And as I mentioned earlier, it's not just for those who live a "sinful" life, either. John, TJ, and their mother are all strong Christians. So, this really is for everyone.

Because I have seen so many "miracles" God does in peoples' lives with this prayer, it has become the *first* thing I share when someone needs help in almost anything — not just for health issues, but practically everything else.

The things we deal with — whether it's arthritis, incurable diseases like Parkinson's or cancer, migraines, *poison*, trauma, PTSD, infertility, or almost anything else — while these things *could* be from purely natural causes, I have found they are often tied to a root of unrepented sin somewhere in our lives.

And what I've experienced over and over again is

that when people repent of specific sins, the health and life challenges they've been dealing with for years often disappear. What's even more remarkable is when those challenges involve physical issues that doctors claim is a normal process of aging — worn-out joints, glaucoma, etc. — God frequently restores all of it back to the way it originally was!

In fact, I was listening to a man speak not long ago. He uses the same process as the Prayer of Freedom, and was sharing three case studies from his personal experience working with people who were paralyzed. In every case, after leading each person through repenting of their sins, each one was completely healed of their paralysis. One of them was even a quadriplegic who had been in a wheelchair for over a year!

This is the whole idea of the next few chapters. Sin *can* cause infirmity, and when an infirmity has an unrepented sin at its root, then repentance can bring about healing.

There's a lot we don't understand spiritually, and one of the things most people don't consider is the direct impact the spiritual realm has on the physical world we live in. And the key behind all of it is... sin. Either we walk in righteousness, or we walk in sinfulness. The Lord wants us to walk in righteousness, and the way to do that is to repent. That's why the primary message Jesus came preaching was, "Repent! For the kingdom of heaven is in your midst."

If you recall from a few chapters back, the word "torture" in the Parable of the Unmerciful Servant comes from the Greek word *basanizo*. And *basanizo* includes either mental suffering, physical suffering (like paralysis), or physical pain. All of these are things we would call "infirmities." An infirmity is anything you would go to the doctor to get help for.

We can see a direct cause of those infirmities in

that parable when Jesus says: "if you don't forgive your brother, my Heavenly Father will turn you over to the torturers..." to bring about *basanizo* discipline until you repent and forgive him.

And here's what's interesting...

If you start searching through both the Old and New Testaments, you'll see direct connections between sin and infirmity (sickness and disease). There are at least *twenty* specific references, and probably as many as forty or fifty. And again, while not all infirmity is caused by sin, what's interesting is when the Bible speaks about causes of infirmities in our lives, it is almost *always* associated with sin.

Let's take a brief walk through just a few of those passages and I'll show you clear, unmistakable links God shows us between sin and infirmity.

If you've never looked at Scripture this way, it will amaze you how clear God has been with us on the reason so many are sick and suffering!

▸ Biblical link between sin and infirmity #1

Our first passage comes from the book of Exodus. As a quick background, this was written just after God freed Israel from Egypt. They crossed the Red Sea and, by this time, they are in the wilderness. God is giving them his laws on how to live. And one of these laws is talking about 'generational iniquity.'

Exodus 34:7 — "[God keeps] steadfast love for thousands, forgiving iniquity and transgression and sin, but who will by no means clear the guilty, <u>visiting the iniquity of the fathers on the children and the children's children to the third and fourth generation</u>." (ESV, clarification added)

If you noticed, there are essentially three types of

sin being talked about here. One is iniquity. Another is transgression. And a third is sin.

To understand what this verse is really saying, it's important to know what each of these sins are. Let's look at them in reverse order...

<u>Sin</u> - The easiest way to understand 'sin' in this context is to think of it as something you do contrary to what God wants you to do, and you do it by accident. Generally speaking, you don't know what you're doing is a sin. That's basically what the Bible is talking about in *this* passage where it has all three categories of sin laid out at the same time. It's talking about an accidental sin — it's what we may often call an "unintentional sin."

<u>Transgression</u> - In simple terms, 'transgression' is when you purposely choose to do what is wrong, rather than to do what you know is right. The actual definition of the word "transgression" is "rebellion."

Have you ever found yourself in a situation where you knew the right thing to do from God's perspective, but your flesh wanted to do something else... and you gave in to your flesh? Your thoughts typically go like this: "I know I really ought to do 'A' [the right thing], because that's what the Lord wants me to do. But I really want to do 'B' [the wrong thing]." For example, maybe you're dating someone. One thing leads to another, and the two of you start sleeping together outside of marriage. You know it's wrong in God's eyes, but you do it anyway. Why? Because you want to.

That's a transgression. It's a sin of rebellion — you know God's desire, but you rebel against Him to fulfill *your* desire.

James 4:17 says it this way, "Whoever knows the right thing to do and fails to do it, for him it is sin." (ESV)

Those are the first two types of sin. But the type of sin I want to focus on is the one that is specifically passed down from one generation to another...

Iniquity - A sin of iniquity is a sin of perversion — it's a *twisting* (or perverting) of God's holy standards. From God's perspective, these are the worst types of sins because they are directly against him and what he has decreed as holy and sacred.

For example, sleeping with someone outside of marriage is a sin of transgression — you know the right thing to do, but you rebel against it and do what you want to do. However, if the person you're sleeping with is the same sex as you, now that becomes a sin of *iniquity*. It's a perversion of God's holy standard and, therefore, a much more serious sin. And why is it a perversion?

Because God states in **Genesis 1:27** that he "created man in his own image... male and female he created them." God's image is holy, and God's standard for Man is that sexual intercourse is to be between a man and a woman only. If a man has sex with a man, or a woman has sex with a woman, it is a perversion of that holy standard and is, therefore, an iniquity.

Other sins of iniquity we frequently see today are things like adultery (twisting God's holy standard of marriage), gender fluidity (twisting God's holy standard of male and female), all forms of witchcraft, worshipping gods of other religions, and much more.

Anything that twists God's holy standard is a sin of iniquity; and it is such a "big" sin that God visits the discipline for it to multiple generations down the line.

If you've ever heard the term 'generational curse,' this is usually what it's talking about. The 'curse' is often a spirit of discipline tied to a sin of iniquity that comes down through the generations. It may look like a pattern of sickness from generation to generation, or abusiveness, or addiction, or anything else. Whatever it looks like, you may start seeing it in your children, too.

And it continues down through the generations *until* that sin is repented of.

And as a reminder, as with all spirits of discipline, God allows them in your life *because* he loves you and wants to bring about repentance.

God wants that sin repented of. And once you repent of it (even if it was committed by a parent or grandparent), the discipline (the "curse") goes away. That's basically the "big idea" of our passage in Exodus.

To help you understand this a little more, think about it this way…

Let's say your mother owned a family heirloom she inherited from her father. When she dies and leaves it to you, that object now becomes *your* object through inheritance. Does that make sense?

This is similar to how a sin of iniquity works, except the person doesn't have to die before you inherit it.

In simplistic terms, if your grandfather on your mother's side commits a sin of iniquity, your mother "inherits" that sin as her own — that's why she receives a spirit of discipline for it. When you are born, it becomes *your* sin, too. Now, you're accountable for it because it passed down through the inheritance of your bloodline. And since you're accountable for it, that same spirit of discipline can torment you.

This is what God means in **Exodus 34:7** when he says, "I will visit the iniquity of the fathers to the third and fourth generation."

But what does it mean to "visit" a sin on future generations?

Well, I've already alluded to it — it appears to be a spirit of discipline in the form of torment that visits us down through our family generations. That's the *basanizo* I mentioned earlier. Addictions coming down, divorce coming down, abuse coming down, sickness coming down, broken relationships coming down, early deaths coming down — we see these patterns, and they all have to do with iniquity.

Recently, I was talking with a friend who doesn't believe in "generational curses" or that God would send pain and suffering to children for their fathers' sins. He claimed I had misinterpreted this passage in Exodus.

I told him Scripture has many examples of this. And here are three examples I shared with him...

The first and most prominent is Adam – **Romans 5:12** (paraphrased) tells us that "death came into the world through Adam's sin, and so death spread to all men."

The second is with King David. After he slept with Bathsheba and murdered her husband, God tells him in **2 Samuel 12:10** (ESV), "the sword shall never depart from your house..."

The third is a passage I'll discuss in more detail in just a moment. After Naaman, the Syrian, had been healed of leprosy, he offered gifts to Elisha, but Elisha refused them. Then, after Naaman left, Elisha's servant, Gehazi, chased him down to receive those gifts as his own. This was a sin. And what did God do? Elisha declares in **2 Kings 5:27** (NIV), "Naaman's leprosy will cling to you and to your descendants forever."

In each of these examples, the fathers' iniquities were visited to their future generations. This is what many people would call a "generational curse," and is exactly what God promised in Exodus 34:7.

And for clarification, when God says, "the iniquities of the *fathers*," he is using an all-encompassing term that means both fathers and mothers.

So, regardless of which branch of the family tree it comes from, any sins of iniquity will come down the line and be visited to future generations until they are repented of. And it doesn't matter what type of sins they are — activity sins, agreement sins, or unholy soul ties (I'll explain these in a later chapter).

Suffice it to say, even though someone else might have committed the sin, it now belongs to you from a "legal rights" standpoint, and it opens you up to a spirit of discipline. The technical term for this is "imputed" — their action is imputed to you, and it is now counted as your action (cf. **Hebrews 7:9**). When they committed a sin of iniquity, that sin is imputed to you through inheritance, and it allows a spirit of discipline to come against you.

On a more positive note, since it is imputed to you, it belongs to you; therefore, *you* can repent of it and stop the discipline in your life and the lives of your children. And the Prayer of Freedom walks you through precisely how to do that.

▶ Biblical link between sin and infirmity #2

Now, let's look at another passage where the Bible connects sin as a cause of infirmity. This passage comes from Moses as he instructs Israel to follow the Lord. It is quite startling...

Deuteronomy 28:58-61 — "If you do not carefully follow all the words in this law, which are written in this book, and do not revere this glorious and awesome Name—the Lord your God—the Lord will send fearful plagues on you and on your descendants, harsh and prolonged disasters, and severe and lingering illnesses. He will bring on you all the diseases of Egypt that you dreaded, and they will cling to you. The Lord will also bring on you every kind of sickness and disaster not recorded in this Book of the Law..." (NIV, emphasis and clarification added)

Look at the correlation here.

"If you do not carefully follow all the words of this law" means "if you disobey and sin against God."

And what happens if you sin against God?

The Lord will send "severe and lingering illnesses. He will bring on you all the diseases of Egypt, every kind of sickness and disaster, and they will cling to you."

That means God will allow infirmity to come upon you, and that infirmity will be chronic ("cling to you") and last a long time. And not *only* infirmity, but other kinds of disaster in your life.

Can it get any clearer? God says, "If you sin against me, I will bring all kinds of infirmity (sickness and disease) and disaster upon you that will go on and on" … *until* you repent.

▸ Biblical link between sin and infirmity #3

Another reference we'll look at ties in with this idea of sin 'clinging' to you. It's the story I mentioned a moment ago about a man named Gehazi who gets leprosy, a condition that rots your skin. Let's read it now…

2 Kings 5:14-16 — "So he [this is talking about a Syrian general named Naaman who had leprosy] went down and dipped himself in the Jordan seven times, as the man of God [Elisha] had told him. And his flesh was restored, and became clean like that of a young boy. Then Naaman and all his attendants went back to the man of God. He stood before him and said, 'Now I know that there is no God in all the world except in Israel. So please accept a gift from your servant.' The prophet answered, 'As surely as the Lord lives, whom I serve, I will not accept a thing.' And even though Naaman urged him, he refused." (NIV, clarification added)

After Elisha refused to take Naaman's gift, Naaman

heads home and goes a short distance before we pick the passage up again in verse 21...

vv. 21, 25-26 — "So Gehazi [Elisha's servant] hurried after Naaman. When Naaman saw him running towards him, he got down from the chariot to meet him. 'Is everything all right?' he asked. 'Everything is all right.' Gehazi answered. 'My master sent me to say [this is a lie, by the way], "Two young men from the company of the prophets have just come to me from the Hill Country of Ephraim. Please give them a talent of silver and two sets of clothing."' 'By all means, take two talents,' said Naaman... When he [Gehazi] went in and stood before his master, Elisha asked him, 'Where have you been Gehazi?' 'Your servant didn't go anywhere,' Gehazi answered. But Elisha said to him, 'Was not my spirit with you when the man got down from his chariot to meet you? Is this the time to take money or to accept clothes—or olive groves and vineyards, or flocks and herds, or male and female slaves?'"

Now, pay attention to this final verse as Elisha continues his message to Gehazi...

v. 27 — "'Naaman's leprosy will cling to you and to your descendants forever.' Then Gehazi went from Elisha's presence and his skin was leprous — it had become white as snow."

Pretty clear and direct, huh? Here we have another *very* straightforward example of sin being the root of an infirmity.

Gehazi commits a terrible sin (receiving gifts by deception for work God did, inferring God's goodness could be purchased with money), and God disciplines him with infirmity — in this case, leprosy that will be passed down from generation to generation. And since it's being "visited" to future generations, we can tell this was a sin of iniquity.

But wait... there's more (as the old infomercials

used to say)!

We start to see even *clearer*, more direct references to the link between sin and infirmity in the New Testament. And if you're like most people, you've probably read these passages and never "connected the dots" on what the Lord was actually showing you.

Read on. I think you'll be surprised!

Chapter 8

Sin is a cause for infirmity (New Testament)

Hanna had been diagnosed with cancer. She and her husband, Jack, are devout Christians, and they believe in the power of God's healing miracles. So they prayed, believing the Lord would heal her, and he did.

God miraculously healed Hanna of cancer! And even when she went back to the doctor, *no* trace of cancer could be found. It had disappeared!

However, the doctor *still* recommended she go through chemotherapy "just in case" it started to come back. Hanna and Jack didn't want to do it; but their adult sons were concerned. They talked to the doctor, and together they pressured Hanna by saying things like, "You should still go through chemo as a back-up. It will be safer that way. We want you to do it."

Because of their insistence, Hanna began to think, "Maybe they're right. After all, you can never be too careful with cancer."

So, going against what she felt in her heart, she started the treatment. And immediately regretted it…

Two years later -

My wife and I were having lunch with my brother and his wife. He started sharing about Hanna and what has happened with her over the past couple of years.

He said, "After she went through chemotherapy, she completely changed. No longer was she that bubbly, fun and full-of-excitement woman I had known.

Instead, she went into a deep, dark depression she couldn't get out of."

For the last two years, Jack had taken her to doctor after doctor; she was put on one prescription after another, and nothing worked. Jack told my brother, "Hanna is no longer the woman I married — she has *completely* changed."

When I heard her story, I instantly recognized this as a spirit of discipline. It was *basanizo* because she sinned against God. God had healed her, and the doctor had confirmed it. But she rejected that healing and, instead, trusted man's opinion over God's truth, believing it might come back.

So, I reached out to her and ultimately led her through the Prayer of Freedom. We prayed together, and she repented of rejecting God's healing and for believing man's opinion.

Within two or three days, all the mental changes she was going through cleared up — the depression left, the anxiety and nervousness left, and mentally she was back to her old self again!

Hanna's story underscores, again, the direct association between sin and infirmity. And in the last chapter I promised to share more biblical passages showing that connection. So now, let's jump into the New Testament to see a few more...

▸ Biblical link between sin and infirmity #4

The previous examples I shared were from the old covenant days — the days of Israel being under the Law. But what about today?

Today, as believers in Jesus, we are no longer under Law in the old covenant. We are under grace in the new covenant. The same issue of sin causing infirmity no longer applies to us, right?

Well, that's not entirely accurate. Sure, lots of things *have* changed for us with the new covenant, but sin no longer being a cause of infirmity is not one of them. Let me show you why.

In First Corinthians, Paul is writing to the church in Corinth. These are believers who were born again and had already put their faith in Jesus. Salvation was already theirs. However, they were a wayward church. There was a lot of sin going on — strife, jealousy, fornication, and more. They were so "bad" Paul ended up writing several letters to them, admonishing and rebuking them each time, trying to correct them.

In this passage, Paul is instructing them about Communion. This is where believers eat the bread and drink from the cup in the presence of others, and "do it in remembrance of" Jesus.

With that backdrop, let's pick up our verse below.

1 Corinthians 11:29 — "For those who eat and drink [talking about taking Communion] without discerning the body of Christ, eat and drink judgment on themselves. <u>That is why many among you are weak and sick, and a number of you have fallen asleep</u>." (NIV, clarification and emphasis added)

When Paul says they were eating and drinking "without discerning the body of Christ," what he means is they were taking Communion in a sinful manner. As you read the text, you'll see they weren't treating it as a holy sacrament. Instead, they were treating it as a personal feast, creating division among the other believers by selfishly ignoring their needs (in those days, Communion was a full meal, not just a wafer and sip of wine or juice as we do today). Because of this, they were bringing judgment on themselves.

In other words, when you take Communion, since it is a "Holy" Communion, you are to do it with a heart of love towards others, the same as Jesus did. You're not to take it in a way that excludes others and creates division, then say, "Okay Lord, bless me. I'm eating and drinking in remembrance of you."

If you do, Paul says you are bringing judgment upon yourself because you are committing a sin when taking Communion. That's what Paul is speaking about here.

And what were the outcomes for the Corinthian _Christians_ when they sinned while taking Communion?

Paul says, "That's why many among you are weak and sick, and a number of you have fallen asleep." The term "fallen asleep" is used here as a euphemism meaning, "they have died."

So, our conclusion from this verse is the same as we've seen with all the others...

Even for Christians who are under the new covenant, sin can be a direct cause of infirmity. And in this case, that infirmity was weakness, sickness, and even death.

"But why? That doesn't seem fair. They're Christians after all. Why did God let that happen to them?"

If that's what you're thinking right now, you're not alone! This is a difficult truth to grasp. And while it may not seem like a loving God would treat us this way, I want to assure you of two things. First, he _does_ allow it. And second, he allows it _because_ he loves us.

If you skip down to verse 32, you'll see what I mean.

1 Corinthians 11:32 — "... when we are judged in this way by the Lord, we are being disciplined <u>so that we will not be finally condemned with the world</u>." (NIV, emphasis added)

There you have it — another reason the Lord disciplines his children: so they _won't_ be condemned when

Christ returns!

It's really the same reason we discipline our own children... so something worse won't happen to them in the future. If they steal candy from their sibling, we discipline them for it. Why? So that later on down the road they won't steal bigger things from someone else and end up in jail.

It makes perfect sense. Discipline is for our good. That's why our Father disciplines us — for our good. We know this because he tells us in **Hebrews 12:10** "God disciplines us for our good, in order that we may share in his holiness."

But it doesn't stop there. Let me share another example...

▸ Biblical link between sin and infirmity #5

I want to take a quick look at the passage in James 5 about calling for the elders if someone is sick. For anyone who has read the Bible, this is a familiar passage; but many people miss a key point James shares with us.

It may seem like this passage is mixing two subjects together — receiving salvation and being healed from sickness — but it's not. James is writing to believers, those who have already confessed they are sinners, have repented of their sins in general, and believe in Jesus. They already have eternal life. Therefore, James is not talking about receiving salvation (i.e. "being saved") in this passage, he's talking about something else.

With that in mind, let's look at what it says:

James 5:14-16 — "Is anyone among you sick? Let him call for the elders of the church, and let them pray over him, anointing him with oil in the name of the Lord. And the prayer of faith will save the one who is

<u>sick</u>, and the Lord will raise him up. And if he has committed sins, he will be forgiven. Therefore, <u>confess your sins to one another</u> and pray for one another, <u>that you may be healed</u>..." (ESV, emphasis added)

Okay, now, let's decipher what this is really saying, and you'll see something amazing. What you'll see is that *sin* is the root of the sickness James is talking about...

v. 14 — "Is anyone among you sick?"

There's the first key. This is talking to *believers* who are sick.

v. 15a — "And the prayer of faith will save the one who is sick..."

That's the second key. Since James is speaking to those who are sick, to "*save* the one who is sick" doesn't mean "receive salvation," as in eternal life. To "save" someone who is sick means to heal them... to save them *from* their sickness.

v. 15b — "... and the Lord will raise him up..."

Again, to "raise" someone up isn't talking about the resurrection due to salvation, it's talking about raising them up from the sick bed.

vv. 15c-16 — "... And if he has committed sins, he will be forgiven. Therefore, confess your sins to one another and pray for one another, that you may be healed."

What will be forgiven? Your sins. And why are they forgiven? Because you confess them (i.e. repent). And what happens when you confess your sins? You are healed.

Now, using those short explanations, let's restate what this passage is actually saying...

"If anyone among you is sick, confess your sins so they may be forgiven and you may be healed."

James is saying it's your *sin* that's causing your sickness, and if you will "confess your sins… you will be healed."

Are you starting to see a pattern with all of these passages?

The understanding from Scripture is clear: <u>sin is a cause of infirmity</u>. And if sin is the cause of *your* infirmity, repenting (confessing) of that sin is the path to being healed.

This is the backbone of the Prayer of Freedom — confessing and repenting of sins that give spirits of discipline a legal right to bring *basanizo* torment to your life. When you do, the discipline stops and you are set free!

But, that's not all the evidence linking sin and infirmity. There's even more. I'll share *that* in the next chapter.

Chapter 9

Sin is still a cause for infirmity today

Since we've been looking at direct links between sin and infirmity in the Bible, I thought it would be a good idea to share a few more examples of sin and infirmity from modern times. The point I want to underscore is that this is not just a "Bible-time" truth. This is ongoing. This is how the Lord's discipline works in our lives; and all we have to do to be freed of the discipline is to *repent*.

And this doesn't apply *just* to infirmity. Spirits of discipline steal, kill and destroy our lives in many ways. Infirmity, relationship problems, economic destruction (job and career issues), and more.

Once I started learning this simple truth, it's been a "game-changer" in ministering to people, regardless of what types of issues they are dealing with.

Read on and see…

▸ Parkinson's disease disappears

A few years back, a friend of mine, Pam, was a hospice care worker. She was working with a lady named Madeline. Madeline was only forty-nine years old at the time. She was in hospice, which means she only had about six weeks or less to live. She was dying of Parkinson's disease, a brain disorder that disrupts your ability to move your muscles, and in advanced stages you feel so weak that you are unable to move. That's where Madeline was.

At the time, Madeline had no strength left. She was so weak the only thing she could move was the pinkie on her right hand. On top of that, she could barely speak above a whisper.

During her visit, Pam asked, "How did you catch Parkinson's disease?"

Madeline whispered, "Oh honey, you can't catch Parkinson's disease. If you could, you wouldn't be in this room with me today." She continued softly, "My husband had Parkinson's; and when he died, I was diagnosed with it."

Pam understood the link between sin and infirmity, so she gently probed, "Did you ever sleep with your husband before you got married?"

Madeline answered, "Yes. What does that have to do with anything?"

Pam explained how pre-marital sex is a sin, and what appeared to be happening was the Parkinson's disease was a spirit of discipline that had been attacking her husband. Then, when he died, *because* of her sex with him before they married, the spirit had a legal right to shift to her... so it did.

At that point, following the pattern of the Prayer of Freedom, Pam led Madeline in a prayer of repentance for that sin, then asked the Lord to remove the Parkinson's disease from her.

When Pam returned to visit Madeline the next week, she was sitting up in bed. All the color had returned to her cheeks and body, and they just had a fun time together, chit-chatting through the whole visit.

The following week when Pam returned, Madeline wasn't there. Pam asked the administrator, "Where's

Pam?" She said, "Oh, she got so much better we discharged her the other day."

Madeline went from 'death row' — about to die on hospice with an incurable disease — to walking out of that place in less than two weeks mostly, if not fully, healed. And it was all because she repented of her sin!

But it's not just Parkinson's, either. Any sickness, even cancer, if its root is unrepented sin, can be reversed.

▸ Addictions, migraines and more disappear

Kathryn is a young woman who had been a drug addict for years. She wrote me this message after doing the Prayer of Freedom. I have edited it for clarity and brevity...

"I want to thank you for the Prayer of Freedom. It has changed my life!

"Growing up, my relationship with my mom was really tough. She was abusive, and she and my stepdad would drink and get into lots of fights. By the time I was in seventh grade, she said she didn't want anything to do with me and left. That's when life began spiraling downward. By sixteen years old, I was having sex with lots of boys and started getting into drugs. That was just over 10 years ago.

"Before doing this prayer, I was addicted to heroin and fentanyl and meth. I had a lot of worry and stress and anxiety. On a scale of 1 to 10, they were probably an 8. I've had constant allergies, sinus headaches and migraines five out of seven days a week, and a super heavy feeling like I was carrying around an overweight backpack every day. Life has really been difficult.

"But the Prayer of Freedom and my repenting changed everything. Literally, everything is gone!

"No more sinus issues. All gone. No more headaches and migraines. All gone. No more heaviness. It's all gone. No more anxiety or stress or worries. Literally, on a scale of 1 to 10, they've all gone to 0. Even my addictions have gone down to 0. I don't want drugs anymore. I have no urges for them anymore. And even the thought of any drug disgusts me. It's all gone!"

All her issues were sin-based. How do I know? Because they all disappeared when she repented of her sins.

I know these stories may sound too good to be true, but the reality is this is exactly what Jesus tells us will happen in **John 10:10** — "The thief comes only to steal, kill and destroy. I came that you might have life, and have it abundantly." (ESV)

The thief only has a legal right to steal, kill, and destroy because of unrepented sin. But **Colossians 2:14-15** tells us Jesus canceled the record of debt for our sins and "disarmed the rulers and authorities" — those "thieves" Jesus talked about — so they no longer have a legal right to attack us.

But the only way we can receive that protection is by faith — by obeying God's command to repent of our sins.

If all of this sounds impossible, just remember that nothing is impossible for God. And when you follow his rules, his promises come true.

It almost sounds too simple, doesn't it?

But yet, it's what the Bible consistently tells us. It says, "confess (i.e. repent of) your sins... that you may be healed."

It really *is* that simple. And it can be that simple for you, too!

Let me share another incredible story to drive the point home even more…

▸ Glaucoma and cataracts disappear

My wife and I had travelled to the Caribbean for a vacation. We had a wonderful time… until it was time to fly home.

We were at the airport, waiting for the plane to land that was supposed to take us back home. But because of bad weather it was delayed, delayed again… then finally canceled. We couldn't leave that day, and had to fly out the next.

To make a long story short, the only hotel we could find with availability was about an hour away. So, we hired a taxi to take us there, and pick us back up again early the next morning to return us to the airport.

As the taxi driver dropped us off at the hotel and was about to leave, I asked him what I typically ask most people — "I pray for people. Before you leave, is there anything I can pray for you about?"

He seemed startled that I would ask, but he said, "Yes, please pray for my eyesight." Then he drove away.

When he picked us up the next morning to take us back to the airport, you could tell something was on his mind. As we were unloading, he said, "I've never had anyone ask if they could pray for me before. You must be a man of God. Do you have time to talk? I have a lot of questions." I said I did. So we went to a coffee shop next door and started talking.

During the conversation, I asked him what was going on with his eyesight. He said he could barely see. And as a taxi driver, that is a *very* important thing to be able to do!

Keep in mind, he had just driven us an hour both ways to and from our hotel. The whole time I was wondering why he had driven so slowly, and why he drove in the *middle* of the road the entire time (except when oncoming traffic passed us). Now I understood!

He said he had cataracts and glaucoma. The cataracts made it difficult to drive at night with oncoming headlights in his eyes, and the glaucoma made it where he could barely see anyway.

There was a giant poster on the wall about fifteen or twenty feet behind me with large words printed on it, and I asked if he could read it. He looked and looked, and squinted... and couldn't read *any* of it.

I then started sharing about the Prayer of Freedom and told him how unrepented sin can cause infirmity. So, I started asking him questions about possible sins he may have committed and, as a 70+ year old man on the island, there were quite a few!

I then led him through an abbreviated version of the Prayer of Freedom. Altogether, it took about twenty minutes. And all I did was guide him in repentance for the various sins the Lord brought to his mind. Then I led him in a prayer, asking the Lord to heal his eyesight. I prayed for him as well, and when it was all over, I asked him to try and read the poster again.

This time, he read the *entire* poster, including the smaller print at the bottom! His eyesight was perfectly restored!

About three weeks after returning home, I reached back out to him and asked how his eyesight was doing. He said that not only was the glaucoma still gone, but also the cataracts — he could see clearly, even with headlights shining in his eyes!

And all of it was simply a spirit of discipline

bringing *basanizo* torment because of unrepented sin.

Why is this so important?

The reason this topic is so important is because many of us (or our loved ones) live with various types of issues and challenges in our lives. We continue to believe they are a normal part of life and there's nothing we can do about them.

But the root cause of many of our issues, whether infirmities or other life challenges, is unrepented sin in one form or another. Not *every* sickness or issue in our life is due to unrepented sin, but from my experience, I've found the vast majority of them are.

That's why it's so vital for us to understand what's going on. Once you understand *why* it happens, you are empowered to get free from it.

Unrepented sin gives spirits of discipline a legal right to attack you. If you want them to stop, all you have to do is remove their legal right to be there. And to do that, all you have to do is repent of the sin that gave it to them in the first place.

There are three types of legal rights that unrepented sin can create. And while the "simple answer" on how to remove the legal right is to repent of that sin, the reality is it's a little more complicated.

Each of the three legal rights requires a slightly different process to break it. If you can't identify which type of legal right a spirit of discipline is using and how to break it, you won't get free of its torment.

In the next chapter, I'll walk you through these legal rights and show you how to nullify each one so you can be set free. So, read on.

Chapter 10

Three types of "legal rights"

bout four years ago a friend of mine handed me a phone number and asked me to pray for a seventy-three year old woman named Francis. I reached out to her, and through our phone conversation learned some fascinating things about this woman.

Francis was a lifelong missionary who had spent the last *fifty years* on the mission field. By all accounts, she had lived a righteous and holy life. But there was one problem.

Francis had been wheelchair-bound and unable to walk for eleven years because of extreme pain in her right foot.

When I asked her what happened, she said, "I had surgery eleven years ago because of some pain in the ball of my foot. The surgery only exacerbated the problem, and the pain got worse. Since then, I've had two more surgeries on it, but the doctors couldn't correct it. So, I've been in a wheelchair ever since."

Based on everything she told me, it just felt like a spirit of discipline. So, I walked her through the steps of the Prayer of Freedom, going through a typical list of sins I've seen with most people.

"Have you ever had sex outside of marriage?" I began. "No," she replied.

"Do you have unforgiveness for anyone?" I asked. Again, she replied, "No."

"Have you ever dabbled in the occult — played with

a Ouija board, participated in a séance, or anything like that?" I asked. Once again, she said, "No."

One after another, everything on my list resulted in a "No." But we needed to get to the bottom of this, so I continued, "Have you ever been part of a secret society or taken any secret oaths?" I asked. "No," she replied.

I was just about to move on to the next question when Francis cut me off excitedly, "Wait! The Lord just reminded me of a secret oath I took a long time ago. I was involved with *Rainbow Girls* in high school and took a secret oath as part of the initiation ceremony. I don't even remember what I said."

Bingo! I thought to myself. Then I said, "I think that might be it. Let's repent of that oath and see what happens."

So, I guided her through a short prayer of repentance, asked the Lord to remove the pain, and I commanded any spirit of discipline that was there to leave immediately. When I did, all the pain in her foot instantly left! And I mean... *instantly*. It was gone. She got out of the wheelchair and started walking with NO pain.

Three months later, I checked back with her, curious to see how things were going. And she confirmed she was still walking normally — no pain, and NO wheelchair!

All it took to free her from the wheelchair was to repent of a sin — a secret, sinful oath she took fifty-three years earlier.

Wow!

For Francis, the oath turned out to be an agreement that was contrary to God's will, and therefore, a sin. It's called an "agreement sin." Let's learn more about it now.

Three types of legal rights

With that, I now want to talk about the three types of "legal rights" unrepented sin creates in our lives. And it's these legal rights that actually give spirits of discipline the authority to torment us.

When you repent of the sin, it sets the stage to remove the legal right. But depending on what type of legal right was created determines how to remove it. And that's what I want to discuss here.

In simple terms, the three legal rights come from (1) Activity Sins, (2) Agreement Sins, and (3) Unholy Soul Ties. Let's look at them one-by-one.

Legal Right #1: Activity Sin

An activity sin is **something you do** that is contrary to God. It's usually a sin of transgression — a rebellion against what God says to do. This could be something like sex outside of marriage, harboring anger or resentment toward another person, or not forgiving someone. Many of the stories I've shared fall under this category.

The discipline for an activity sin will continue for as long as you live. To stop the discipline from an activity sin, you must **repent** of the sin.

Legal Right #2: Agreement Sin

An agreement sin is an **agreement you make** that is contrary to God. Agreement sins are sins of iniquity — they are a perversion, or twisting, of God's holy standards.

Many of the agreement sins I've worked with had entered the peoples' lives when someone — either them or an ancestor — had taken an oath that was unknowingly contrary to God.

This is what happened with Francis. She wanted to join *Rainbow Girls* (a subset of *Freemasons*) because it sounded like a lot of fun. As part of the initiation ceremony, she had to repeat a secret oath. She didn't really understand what it all meant — in fact, it probably sounded a little weird at the time — but she played along and repeated it. Why? Because they were only words, right? What she didn't realize is part of that oath created an agreement sin that would come back to haunt her years later in life.

As far as the discipline goes, though, unlike an activity sin where the discipline is only directed toward you, the discipline for an agreement sin continues until the agreement is broken — that means it can last not only for as long as *you* live, but it can also be passed down to your children and their children as well.

In other words, agreement sins are sins of iniquity, and God visits the discipline for them to the third and fourth generations. A lot of times, when people see this discipline impacting one generation after another, they consider it a "family curse" because it doesn't stop. As I mentioned earlier, this is usually where you hear the term "generational curse." But in reality, a generational curse is nothing more than a spirit of discipline coming down through the generations because of a sin of iniquity.

To stop the discipline from an agreement sin, instead of repenting of the sin like you do with an activity sin, you must **renounce** the agreement that created the sin.

▶ Secret societies and secret oaths

There are many ways people commit agreement sins. The root of all agreement sins is simply believing something contrary to God's holy standard. Because you believe it, you agree with it. And because you agree with it, you act on it. When you do, it's a perversion and twisting of his standard.

There are many examples of agreement sins I could share — adultery, abortion, same-sex marriage, gender fluidness, worship of other gods, all forms of witchcraft (including Wicca and other forms of "white magic"), and more. But the common thread with all of these is they pervert and twist God's holy standards.

However, there is one way people either "inherit" or commit agreement sins today that most people don't really understand. That is by taking "secret" oaths as part of a secret society. This is especially true in the Western world where secret societies have been prominent for hundreds of years.

Because of the widespread presence of secret societies, plus the fact most people misunderstand the impact that "secret" oaths can carry, I want to take a moment to talk about them.

For clarity, a "secret society" is any organization where members are required to take certain oaths of secrecy. Many secret societies are seen as positive, community-focused organizations that do great projects to help others. As an example, two of the more prominent secret societies most people have heard of are *Freemasons* and *Shriners*. Both of these, as with others, have a strong focus on Christian fellowship and giving back to their communities. And because of that, they have widespread respect.

I personally have several friends who are either directly engaged in Freemasonry or have ancestral connections to them. And most of these friends are out-standing Christians.

Take my friend Jeff, for instance. He's a devout, born-again Christian, deeply committed to mentoring men in need. He has an intimate walk with the Lord, a deep theological understanding of God's word, and dedicates significant time each week to guiding under-privileged men in learning God's Word. As a result, he is significantly changing their lives. And, as a Freema-son, many of his closest Christian friends are members of his lodge. They have great fellowship and worship God together there.

The "issue," if I can call it that, with secret societies isn't the members themselves. Instead, it lies in the fact that some of the oaths they are required to recite inad-vertently create agreement sins.

A lot of times, those oaths may appear somewhat odd or even amusing. While going through one of the ceremonies you might think, "This is a little weird, but I'll go along with it," and recite an oath without thinking about what it really means. However, from a spiritual perspective, a single sentence within one of those oaths might be *significantly* contrary to God. And, if you don't fully understand what you're agreeing to, you might do what Francis did in high school and, unknowingly, cre-ate an agreement sin that plagues you and your family for years to come.

Here's a simple example…

In all secret societies, members commit to keeping their oaths and passwords secret from the "outside world." This initially seems reasonable. However, a portion of the secrecy oaths usually involve agreeing to maintain that secrecy under the threat of extreme pun-ishment, like death or dismemberment.

For instance, some oaths may include the phrase, "I agree to keep these oaths and passwords secret under the penalty of having my throat slit, my chest cut open, and my beating heart ripped out." Then, to emphasize it, they use hand motions of slitting their throat, or motions of ripping open their chest and pulling out their heart.

That's a pretty gruesome oath, isn't it?

Nevertheless, many members see it as childish and whimsical, especially in the context of "intrigue" during a mysterious ceremony, so they agree to it. Why? Because it's a requirement for membership. After all, they don't really mean it. There's no harm in just repeating a few words, right?

Yet, God doesn't see it that way. For him, it is sin.

Additional oaths usually require you to agree to things such as, "I enforce this commitment on my descendants and generations to come," while other oaths may proclaim loyalty and devotion to "the Great Architect of the universe." These might appear innocuous at first glance, but it's the hidden implications that pose the danger. From a Christian perspective, swearing allegiance to "the Great Architect of the universe" might resemble a commitment to Almighty God as the universe's creator. However, "the Great Architect of the universe" isn't talking about God; it's a title for Satan! What's more, by making oaths like these, you could inadvertently bind your descendants and future generations to whatever curses you agreed to.

It's little nuances like these that make "secret" oaths so insidious.

Once more, I'm not judging or criticizing the *people* involved in these organizations. A number of my friends are members of them and, as I mentioned, I love and respect them. The concern is some of the oaths unknowingly create agreement sins. And those sins give spirits of discipline a legal right to you and your descendants.

And even if *you* aren't involved in secret societies personally, because they have been so prevalent for hundreds of years, an ancestor such as a great-great-grandfather may have been involved. If he was, and if he took these types of oaths, you may not know anything about it. Even so, some of the issues you are experiencing now *could* be directly tied to what he did a hundred years ago.

This is why I can't stress it enough; *any* "secret" oath can be dangerous.

But if an ancestor *did* take some of these types of oaths that you know nothing about, don't worry, the Prayer of Freedom handles it automatically.

▶ Patterns of discipline

Recognizing discipline from agreement sins is usually easy, especially if it was something one of your ancestors did. All you have to do is look for patterns, either in your life or coming down your family line. The pattern you're looking for is usually some form of *destruction*. If you see a pattern of destruction, there's a good chance there's a spirit of discipline tied to an agreement sin that's behind it.

For example, addiction is a *big* pattern you'll see. When I work with people struggling with addictions, I'll ask them to raise their hands if their parents or grandparents struggled with addictions as well. And guess what — 80% of them raise their hands! Addiction is often a spirit of discipline tied to an agreement sin. That means if you want to get rid of the addiction, you must first renounce the agreement.

But addiction is just one of many patterns you'll find. Other patterns may be abuse, divorce, anxiety, asthma, early death, suicide, and more. Doctors will typically say, "You are genetically *pre-disposed* to such-

and such an issue," but they are only looking at it from a physical perspective. On a spiritual level, you'll often find the *true* source of the issue is an unrepented sin, and in this case, an agreement sin.

How do I know?

Because the Prayer of Freedom will often get rid of those issues. And if it *does*, it's because it was a spirit of discipline.

▶ My own battle with Agreement Sins — from 150 years ago!

I'm one of those who had been plagued by a spirit of discipline from past agreement sins and never knew what was going on. But then, I started recognizing an unmistakable pattern in my life.

I started my business twenty-five years ago at the time I'm writing this. When I first started my business, the Lord blessed it and it grew extremely fast. But then, something happened. We hit a peak and my business collapsed. I grew it again, and it crashed again. For the next twenty-three years, I felt like I was on a roller coaster. My business would grow and make money, and then it would come crashing back down. One time was so bad I almost went bankrupt.

I knew I couldn't be *that* incompetent in business, but there was no other answer. It felt like someone was sabotaging everything I did. Then something happened to convince me that was *exactly* what was happening!

At the time, I was trying to grow my sales team. I needed one more sales rep. And over a period of two years I hired *thirty* new sales reps — not all at once, but one at a time. And every time I'd hire a new rep, between two weeks before starting to two weeks after starting, a significant "life issue" would come up in their life that would cause them to quit. So, I'd have to start all over again from scratch — interview more candidates, make another hiring decision, and hire another rep.

This *literally* happened for thirty salespeople in a row. And all thirty reps — 100% of them — had a significant, personal issue happen after I hired them... between two weeks of starting to two weeks after starting. And every single time, they quit!

I was desperate for help. I asked the Lord to reveal what was going on and how to stop it. That's when he sent a friend named Barbara into my life. She was experienced in these types of issues and helped identify a spirit of discipline coming down my family line because of an agreement sin.

Through prayer, God not only revealed it was a spirit of discipline tied to an agreement sin, but that the agreement sin was the sin of slavery.

Over 150 years ago, my great-great-great-grandfather was a plantation owner with lots of slaves. Enslaving people against their will is an atrocious sin, so bad it's one of the few sins in the Old Testament punishable by death (**Exodus 21:16**). It was because of this sin that a spirit of discipline was coming down my family line and attacking me.

Also, since spirits of discipline usually operate in a similar nature as the sin that gave them their legal right, that is exactly what was happening in my life. Slavery is a sin focused on economic gain; therefore, the discipline coming down was one of economic destruction. That's what I was experiencing.

Once I realized what it was and why, with Barbara's help I repented of those sins, renounced the agreements tied to them, and asked the Lord to remove the discipline from my life. When I did, everything changed!

For years, running my business had felt like

navigating a ship in a raging storm, just trying to keep it afloat. Then, within about three months after praying the Prayer of Freedom, the storm ceased and the waters went calm. I went from high stress to no stress; from worrying about the business with no rest in sight, to breathing a sigh of relief and the ability to rest and move forward.

Legal Right #3: Unholy Soul Ties

The final type of legal right is what's known as an "unholy" soul tie. While you won't find this term explicitly in the Bible, it is inferred. But even though it's only inferred, in practical, real-life experience, you can clearly see its existence when dealing with the Prayer of Freedom.

Unholy soul ties are a bit tricky because they involve another person in one way or another. They are formed when either an activity sin or an agreement sin is committed **between you and another person**. It's essentially a spiritual connection between you and the other person. This connection is a doorway — a legal right — which gives a spirit of discipline that has a legal right to the other person to now have a legal right to you as well.

What's also unique about this type of legal right is the sin that creates the unholy soul tie does not have to be consensual. It frequently is, but it doesn't have to be. The only thing needed to create an unholy soul tie is the *presence* of sin between you and someone else.

For example, sex outside of marriage always creates an unholy soul tie with the other person. Doing drugs with someone else, or buying drugs from another person, creates an unholy soul tie with that person. But even if you did not agree to the sin — maybe you were abused by someone else — simply the fact that a sin was committed against you can still create an unholy soul tie.

Unholy soul ties remain legal rights for spirits of discipline to attack you until you **break** them.

And here's the "tricky" part about unholy soul ties…

Even if you repent of the sin you committed with the other person, thereby canceling that sin's legal right, the unholy soul tie still remains as a separate legal right until you *break* it as well. On top of that, unholy soul ties remain as a legal right for as long as *you* live, even if the other person has died.

The best way to explain how it works is with another story…

▸ Breaking cigarette addiction

A friend was sharing with me about a friend of hers named Julie. Julie is a strong Christian who was addicted to cigarettes. She tried everything to stop smoking, but still smoked three packs of cigarettes a day. Nothing helped.

Julie had followed the precepts of the Prayer of Freedom — she repented of all the sins the Lord reminded her of, she repented of smoking and hurting her body (God's temple), and more. But she still couldn't quit. Something was still inciting her to smoke.

Then. one day while speaking with a pastor, the pastor asked, "Have you broken the unholy soul tie with the person who taught you to smoke?" Julie said, "No." The pastor then asked about who taught her how to smoke. Julie responded, "It was my babysitter from when I was ten years old. She taught me to smoke and gave me my first pack of cigarettes."

The pastor then guided her through breaking the

unholy soul tie with that babysitter, and asked the Lord to remove the spirit of addiction.

He did, and Julie walked out of the pastor's office never smoking another cigarette since!

Recap

Before closing out this chapter, let's recap a few things...

First, activity sins are things you *do*, and to stop the discipline you **repent** of the sin.

Second, agreement sins are things you *agree to*, and to stop the discipline you **renounce** the agreement.

Third, unholy soul ties are spiritual connections between you and another person when sin is committed *between* the two of you, and to stop the discipline you **break** the soul tie.

All three of these create "legal rights" for spirits to bring discipline into your life. That discipline is usually in the form of *basanizo* — physical suffering, mental suffering, or physical pain. But it can also manifest in other ways, such as abusiveness from someone else, addictions, constant life failures in work or relationships, economic destruction (as happened with me), and more.

Regardless of the *form* of the discipline, God set up the spiritual laws that allow the discipline to happen for a reason — because he *loves* you and wants you to repent of your sin so you can conform more to the image of his Son.

If you've been struggling with things that just don't make sense and you can't seem to get rid of them — fibromyalgia, arthritis, headaches, sickness, heaviness, rage, relationship failures, work or career failures, whatever it is — in almost every case, when you see a pattern that is chronic and doesn't stop, it is most likely a spirit of discipline. And that spirit of discipline is *always* tied to an unrepented sin.

If you have *multiple* issues occurring, it's almost certain you have *multiple* unrepented sins that are the root cause of what's going on.

And if you or a loved one is dealing with some of the 'woke' ideology issues that are running rampant today — gender identity, sexual perversions, and all other forms of extreme evil — you'll find the root of all of these is an accumulation of deep, unrepented sin. Because of that, the Prayer of Freedom can help in those situations, as well.

And while I'm on this subject, let me suggest something...

All of us, including our spouses and children, have struggles in our lives. Many are tied to unrepented sin. And often, we don't recognize it for what it is.

Because of that, I recommend giving your spouse and children their own copy of *The Prayer of Freedom* book. As you're about to see in Section 2, each book includes its own worksheets to use with the prayer. One is to make a list of unrepented sins for which you need to repent. The other is to track the results the Lord brings to your life.

If each family member has their own copy, it will be easier for them to use the worksheets and do the prayer. You can get copies at any bookstore, by scanning the QR code on the cover of this book, or use this link: www.**ThePrayerOfFreedom*Book*.com**.

Ready for a change?

If you struggle to believe all of this — if it sounds too good to be true or too simple to handle your problems — that's okay. Just don't let it stop you from doing the prayer. You don't have to believe it for God to bring freedom to your life. You just have to repent. So, try it. You have nothing to lose... and a world of freedom to gain!

And to give you encouragement, I want to share the testimony and issue grid from Bernice. She was one of my students where I volunteer teach, and her results are encouraging to see.

What I want you to see is how, after her first week, very little changed in her life. But by the fourth week, the problems she had been struggling with had almost fully melted away and she felt like a new person. And within a few more weeks of doing the Prayer of Freedom, I believe most everything in her life will have completely disappeared.

Here's her story, edited slightly for clarity...

Bernice's story

"I had many unrepented sins from the time I was a child to today, everything from sexual abuse as a child to many others. And I've been suffering with all kinds of aches and pains in my body.

"Growing up, I had a big family. My mother and father were already divorced twice by the time I was three years old. She remarried, and my stepfather had five children and my mother had five. Then, by the time I was twelve they adopted my sister's baby, so my mother had her hands full.

"It was at that time I was sexually abused by the

youth minister at the church we belonged to, and my parents began verbally abusing me, too. I thought I deserved everything I got and how I was being treated. It was also at this time that I started to trade my body for drugs, and pornography started to become a big part of my life.

"Since then, I've been diagnosed with two types of bipolar disorder, PTSD, depression, anxiety, and lots of medical issues including COPD and neuropathy.

"I've had three strokes, RLS, and blocked arteries three times in my left foot. I've also attempted suicide and almost succeeded. I was a full blown alcoholic, then started smoking ice, then moved on to crack cocaine.

"My life has been in a downward spiral for a very long time. That's where I was when you shared the Prayer of Freedom with me.

"When I started doing the prayers, I didn't feel much of a difference in anything.

"But then, as the days and weeks passed, I could feel things starting to change. The thoughts in my head were more of God, and a soothing peace of mind started to flood over me.

"I'm still working on some of these, but for the most part I feel completely different. I feel so much lighter, like a *brand new* person!

"Thank you, Mr. Carmichael, for teaching me this method, and thank you Jesus for helping to heal my soul."

While her story shares a lot of what's been going on in her life, when you look at her issue grid (similar to what you'll find in Chapter 11) you'll see how much she had been dealing with. You'll also see how powerful the Prayer of Freedom has been in melting it all away!

Turn the page now to review it.

Bernice's issue grid

Issue	Scale of 0-10, with 10 = worse		
	BEFORE the Prayer	AFTER 1 Week	AFTER 4 Weeks
Heaviness (feels like you are carrying around a heavy backpack every day)	10	8	2
Darkness (seems like your mind or life is dark)	10	↓	2
Mental torments (list below, such as depression, anxiety, voices in head, etc)	10		2
bipolar- type 1 and 2	10	9	2
depression	10		3
anxiety	10		3
Voiceces in my head	10		3
Mom and Dad / Youth min.	10		3
Pain or Stiffness (list below what type of pain or stiffness, such as back pain, chest pain, stiff left knee, etc)	10	↓	3
Block artiries in my Car	10		3
arthuritis in both hips	10	9	3
Knee pain	10		2
Back pain	10		3
restless leg	10	↓	
Sicknesses / illnesses (list below what type, such as asthma, allergies, bipolar, etc)	10		3
bipolar	10	9	4
Copd	10		4
Nueropathy	10	↓	3
RLS	10		2
Addiction (list below any addictions you suffer with, such as drugs, alcohol, pornography, etc)	Rate the level of your urges		
drugs	0	6	0
pornography	10	8	0
cigaretts	10	10	10

Hopefully, your life hasn't been as difficult as Bernice's. Her life is an extreme example and she's had lots of problems to deal with. But the good news is: if the Prayer of Freedom can free her from *her* problems, it can free you from *yours*, too!

So, if *you* are ready for a change — ready to get free of whatever issues are in your life — then the time has come. Take the next step and start the Prayer of Freedom process in Section 2.

In Section 2, we'll start looking at the Prayer of Freedom and how to apply it. And not only how to do it for yourself, but how you can pray it on behalf of your children, spouse, and even parents, to help set them free.

So, if you (or a child, spouse, or parent) suffer with health issues, emotional pain, psychological trauma, addictions, or any other life challenge, there *may* be a root of unrepented sin at its core. And if there is, your freedom *is* possible!

Let's begin…

– Section 2 –

The Prayer
and Next Steps

Chapter 11

The first steps to getting free

Now, let's talk about the Prayer of Freedom. In just a moment, I'm going to share it with you and teach you how to use it. But before I do, you need to understand that it is most effective if you are a "born again" Christian.

A "born again" Christian is one who has confessed that he or she is a sinner and believes in Jesus for salvation — believes that Jesus died on the cross for their sins.

If you have not made that type of confession for Jesus to become your Lord and Savior, the Prayer of Freedom won't work for you. However, don't worry. It's easy to have that relationship if you want it. Let me explain...

In case you don't know much about who Jesus is, let me share what the Bible tells us about him.

In simple terms, the Bible tells us that all of us have sinned and fall short of God's glory. That's what I meant earlier when I said, "sin breaks the relationship with God" and "sin breaks the image of God." However, because we are unable to pay the penalty for our sin, God sent his Son, Jesus, to pay the penalty for us.

That happened about 2000 years ago. Jesus was a person just like you and me except for two things: he was completely sinless, and he was fully God.

Jesus even tells us why he came in **Luke 4:18** (paraphrased). He said it was "to proclaim good news to the poor, to proclaim freedom for the prisoners, recovery of sight for the blind, and to set the oppressed free." In other words, everything I've been sharing so far.

How did Jesus do that?

He lived a perfect life, never sinning even one time. Then, he was crucified on a cross (a Roman method of execution) and died. God used his death — the death of God's sinless Son — to pay the penalty for our sins. The Bible says he "bore our sins in his body on the cross, so that we might die to sin and live for righteousness." (**1 Peter 2:24**, NIV)

After he died, he was buried. Then, three days later he came back to life and rose from the grave, proving that death had no power over him and showing that he has the power to free us from eternal death, too. Today, he sits in heaven with God.

Jesus did all of that for you and me — to pay the penalty for our sins (yours, mine, and everyone else's). But here's the catch: you don't get "credit" for his paying the penalty for your sins *unless* you believe in him and what he did.

The Bible says, "Believe in the Lord Jesus and you shall be saved." (**Acts 16:31**, paraphrased)

So, if you have never made a personal commitment to Jesus by confessing your sins and believing in him to receive salvation, and you would like to be "born again" spiritually, then all you have to do is pray a simple prayer like this...

"Lord Jesus, I confess I'm a sinner. I repent of my sins. Please forgive me. I want your freedom from all these spirits of discipline against me. Please come into my life right now. I surrender my life to you and choose to follow you as my Lord. Amen."

That's it — just a simple, heartfelt prayer. But it's not the words of the prayer that make it work, it's your commitment expressed through those words.

If you prayed that prayer for the first time and meant it, that means you are now "born again" into the family of God. And if you did, you probably feel a tremendous sense of peace and joy flooding over you right now. That peace and joy is God's Holy Spirit coming upon you and starting to change your life.

So, welcome to the family!

Now, let's talk about the Prayer of Freedom. There are a few more things to understand before I share the prayer itself...

Abbreviated Process vs. Complete Process

There are two ways to do the Prayer of Freedom — a quick, Abbreviated Process; and a longer, Complete Process.

Since the prayer's entire focus is to repent of individual, specific sins, the **Complete Process** is most effective. In this process, you first take time to write out a list of *all* unrepented sins the Lord brings to your attention (to help with this, I have included a **List Preparation Guide** in the Appendix of this book). Once you've completed that step, you pray through the Prayer of Freedom, using your list to repent of those sins.

The upside to this process is it's extremely thorough. Because of that, you're likely to identify every potential sin giving a legal right to spirits of discipline in your life so you can get completely free. The downside is it takes more time to create your list — usually around an hour or more.

The second way to do the prayer is the **Abbreviated Process**. Rather than taking time to make a list of sins in your life, with this approach you simply jump in and start praying the Prayer of Freedom. When the Lord prompts you to repent of various types of sins, simply repent of the sins that immediately come to mind.

The upside to this process is it's quick and easy, and you can do it right now without taking any time to prepare. And even though it is abbreviated, you should still see noticeable results.

However, the downside is a lot of things may be missed, and you'll probably want to come back and redo it again later using the Complete Process.

So, which method should you choose?

I share both options because some people have less severe issues than others. And if you are fortunate enough to have only minor issues — maybe just a low-grade migraine every now and then — you might find the Abbreviated Process will handle them fine. And if you go that route and see it working, but some issues remain, you can always return and do the Complete Process later.

In wrapping up this section, I'd like to share a story...

I have a friend named Bob. He was having tough times while going through a nasty divorce. He came over, and in conversation I simply led him through the Abbreviated Process. It was like, "Okay, repent of anyone you have unforgiveness for... repent of this... and repent of that," and we just went through it "off the cuff." Even doing it that way, the changes were immediate.

When I asked him about it later, he said, "After the prayer, I felt heat and light fill my body, and like 100 pounds were lifted off my shoulders. All the stress in my body, and all the butterflies in my stomach, totally disappeared!"

Later on, though, the Lord prompted him to take the time to go through the Prayer of Freedom again, this time doing the Complete Process. So, he did.

He told me that he went back through it a second time using the List Preparation Guide and made a list of all the additional sins he missed the first time around. When he went back through it again, he said the *increased* change was as significant as it was the first time — he got even *more* freedom!

With that being said, depending on the severity of issues you want to be freed of, you can certainly benefit from doing the Abbreviated Process right now. But if you take the time to do the Complete Process by working through the List Preparation Guide first, you'll experience a far more dramatic change.

How fast will this work?

People often ask, "How fast will the Prayer of Freedom work?" My response is always, "It depends."

I've seen some get freedom from their issues in one day. For others, it may take a week, a month, or possibly longer, depending on what's going on.

To help put it in better perspective, let me share a survey I did. And in case you missed it in the "About This Book" section, it's worth repeating here...

I do volunteer teaching at a women's addiction recovery center. As you might imagine, those ladies are dealing with all kinds of issues in their lives — addictions, depression, anxiety, bipolar disorder, anger issues, abuse, trauma, and much more. While preparing to write this book, I wanted to statistically measure how effective this prayer is, so I did a survey with them.

I had each of them in my classes write a list of issues they were dealing with in their lives, then rate each issue on an intensity scale to indicate how bad it was. Next, I had them go through the Complete Process with the Prayer of Freedom, starting with the List Preparation Guide and making detailed lists of all the sins the Lord prompted them of. Once they did that and had completed the prayer, they updated me on what happened in their lives. Here's what their data showed…

Nearly 9 out of 10 (90% of my students) received *significant* relief from their issues, while the remaining 1 out of 10 reported only minimal relief.

Of the 90% who received significant relief, here's a deeper look at their actual results. Now keep in mind, these ladies had *a lot* of issues going on in their lives, much more than your average person. Most of them had been abused or abandoned, many had lived on the streets, and most had been living with multiple addictions and all the associated issues that come along with them for years. Even with the accumulation of all these problems, all but *one* saw almost *all* of their issues **completely disappear** — 100% relief of everything from mental torment (heaviness, depression, bipolar disorders, anxiety); addiction urges (for drugs, alcohol, pornography, and sex); all kinds of physical maladies and pain they had been suffering with for years; all of it… gone!

And then, for those few issues that still remained, the average intensity had been reduced to about *one-third* of their original levels before beginning the prayer (this is what you saw on Bernice's issue grid I shared at the end of Chapter 10).

That doesn't mean those remaining issues *won't* go away. It just means that by the end of the survey time — about one month — some issues still remained. But with continued prayer, the majority will continue to melt away and disappear, too.

What I've learned with this process is if your issues are rooted in unrepented sin, then once you repent of those sins and ask the Lord to remove the spirits of discipline, they will leave. That's why my biggest encouragement to you when going through this process is to be persistent, patient, and give it time.

Making the Prayer of Freedom work for YOU

While I don't fully understand why some people or issues take longer than others to get freedom, my guess is it has something to do with four keys that make the Prayer of Freedom work. If you do these properly, it will work more effectively for you.

First, you must pray the Prayer of Freedom *out loud*. Spirits of discipline need to know you have repented of the sins giving them a legal right to you. But, since they can't hear your thoughts, you must pray aloud so they can hear your voice. However, you don't have to speak so loudly that everyone in the house can hear you. Spirits hear extremely well, so all it takes is a soft whisper.

Second, you must engage the Prayer of Freedom with a heart of repentance and faith. If you truly repent and pray in faith, the prayer will work. If you simply read the words but it's not from your heart, then it won't work. It's not the words of the prayer that work. It's the attitude of your heart, being guided through the words, that makes it work. And the attitude of the heart that's needed is one of repentance and faith. When those two ingredients are present, the Prayer of Freedom will work for you.

Third, you must repent of the specific sins that give spirits of discipline a legal right to you. If you miss the sins for which you are being disciplined, the discipline won't go away. So be thorough when making your lists.

Fourth, visualize what you're praying. In other words, if you simply read the words of the prayer but aren't really focused on what you're saying — maybe your mind is wandering to other things — the prayer won't be as effective. However, if you "visualize" the words as you pray them — meaning you actively focus and concentrate on them — your prayer will be more effective because it will be prayed with greater faith (faith is seeing what is not seen, and that has significant power when praying).

One way to do this is to read the prayer slowly enough that you can concentrate and focus on the words you're saying. If you speed read it out loud, you're usually focused only on reading rather than praying, and that will make it less effective.

Don't change the combination

Another important part of this prayer that makes it work is the "combination."

Imagine for a moment you're standing in front of a giant, bank-sized vault with a large combination lock in the center. Inside the vault are all the blessings the Lord has promised for your abundant life.

If you don't know the combination, you can't open the vault to get your blessings. But the Lord has given you the combination. It's the Prayer of Freedom.

I won't sugar-coat it. The Prayer of Freedom is a BIG prayer. It's a group of three, long, separate prayers, each with its own focus and purpose. And without trying to sound too "spiritual" about it, the Lord actually directed me, over a period of months, exactly how to put it together. In other words, he guided me through the "combination" to unlock the vault. And that combination *works*!

So, what's the combination?

As I was putting the prayer together I had no

knowledge of any "combination." But once it was all finalized, the Lord showed me the combination and its "holiness." It is a set of three numbers, with each number being a holy number...

3-33-70.

There are **3** separate prayers, each with a specific purpose. They are prayed over **33** days, for a total of **70** individual prayer sessions.

So, even though it's a BIG prayer and it takes a *long* time to pray through it, don't change the combination by trying to short-cut the process. Follow the Lord's combination as he gave it and allow it to unlock the vault to your freedom!

However, there is one exception to this rule...

If you struggle with problems that you need *immediate* freedom from, then rather than praying these prayers over the normal, 33-day period of time, you can squeeze them all into a single day and it will be nearly as effective.

If you plan to do it this way, though, be sure to pray each prayer the specified number of times for the full 70 prayer sessions. And between the List Preparation Guide and the 70 prayer sessions, it will likely take six to eight hours to complete, so plan accordingly.

Instructions

We're almost there! At this point, just before you start praying the Prayer of Freedom, I encourage you to do what I did with my students. Make a list of all the issues in your life. Rate each one on an intensity scale of 0 to 10 (10 being the highest). Then, after completing the Prayer of Freedom, review your list and re-rate the intensity of each item. This will be a great encouragement to you as you see what God does in your life. I have included a grid on the next page for you to make your list.

And because agreement sins from your life (or those of your ancestors) may also be impacting your children, I have included a second grid to complete on their behalf. This will help you measure the overflow impact the Prayer of Freedom has on *their* lives as well.

Once you complete the following issue grids, then continue to the next chapter and begin the Prayer of Freedom.

Issue grid for YOU

List everything you struggle with, such as migraines, depression, addiction, anxiety, anger, PTSD, aches and pains, infertility, etc. Then rate the intensity level *now* before praying. After completing Prayer #2, rate the intensity level of each item. Then, after completing the 30 days of Prayer #3, rate the intensity level of each item again. Tracking what the Lord does in your life will be a great encouragement to both you and anyone you choose to share it with.

Scale 0 to 10 (10 = highest)

Issue	Before Praying	After Prayer 2	After Prayer 3

Issue grid for your CHILDREN

List and rate everything your children struggle with, including behavior problems.

Scale 0 to 10 (10 = highest)

Child's Name and Issue	Before Praying	After Prayer 2	After Prayer 3

Chapter 12

The Prayer

I f you do the Complete Process, your *first* step before praying the Prayer of Freedom is to do the **List Preparation Guide** found in the **Appendix** at the end of this book. This is the *most* important step if you want the best results.

The List Preparation Guide is a step-by-step process that walks you through various categories where you might have unrepented sins. It's like a "memory jogger" to help you remember sins you may have forgotten about over time.

Additionally, as you write out your lists, you do it in partnership with the Lord, asking him to remind you of everything you need to repent of to be set free. The most wonderful thing about it is, since he wants you to be free, he will *always* reveal the sins you need to repent of.

Then, once you finish the List Preparation Guide (or if you skip it and jump directly to the Abbreviated Process), the next step is to **start the prayer**. The Prayer of Freedom is divided into three prayers. Here's what they are...

Prayer #1 is to repent of Activity Sins, break unholy soul ties, and command all spirits of discipline to leave. You only need to pray this prayer one time.

Prayer #2 is to renounce Agreement Sins. This is a special prayer you will pray three times a day for three days. The "three times a day" can be done in any format you'd like — either pray it three times in a row in one sitting, or pray it once in the morning, once at midday, and once in the evening. You'll actually start this the same day you do Prayer #1, but Prayer #2 will continue for the next three days.

Prayer #3 is a "final cleanup" prayer you will pray twice a day for thirty days *after* you've completed the three days of Prayer #2. This prayer reinforces the previous prayers and continues to ask the Lord to remove all remaining spirits of discipline from your life.

Now, you're finally ready to begin the Prayer of Freedom! Just follow the instructions.

Please note: if you are doing the Abbreviated Process, when the prayer directs you to repent of sins on your list, just repent of whatever sins the Lord places on your heart for that category.

Note: If you are reviewing this as a possible solution for someone else and you don't plan to do the prayer section, please jump ahead and continue reading the final chapters, Chapters 13 through 15.

Prayer #1
Repent of **Activity Sins**

Pray **one** time. Pray **out loud.**

Lord Jesus, I repent of my sins, and I thank you for dying on the cross for me. I accept your covering of my sins with your blood, and I claim my freedom from the curse of sin and torment that you have promised.

I choose to forgive others — everyone who has hurt me, lied to me, or disappointed me, I forgive them. I repent of unforgiveness; I know it is sin. I put it under the blood of Jesus. I repent of anger, bitterness, hatred, rebellion, resentment and revenge, envy, jealousy and strife, lust, witchcraft, idolatry, and all the works of the flesh. I put it all under the blood of Jesus, and by doing so I break Satan's power and legal rights to my life. I repent of the sins in my bloodline that I inherited through my mother and father. I break the power of generational curses and word curses, and deny permission of any contrary spirit in my life. I repent of and denounce any contract with Satan that impacts my life that either I or anyone else has made; since he is a liar, no contract is binding. By your blood, Lord Jesus, I free myself from any pact with the devil. I renounce all unholy oaths, vows, pledges, and ceremonies that either I or my ancestors have made. I confess as sin, renounce, and break all unholy soul ties.

I repent of all unrighteous bloodshed in my ancestral line; all sins of divination, whether known or unknown; witchcraft; and other forms of occultic activities that I or my ancestors have committed; and by the blood of Jesus I break the power of Divination and all other powers over me.

And I repent of the following sins and lay them all under your blood...

1. Childhood Parent Relationship

For father - I forgive my father for (*name each "father" item on List 1: Parent Relationship*). Those things wounded me. I forgive him, release all judgments against him, and break all unholy soul ties with him.

For mother - I forgive my mother for (*name each "mother" item on List 1: Parent Relationship*). Those things wounded me. I forgive her, release all judgments against her, and break all unholy soul ties with her.

For grandparents - I forgive my grandparents for (*name each "grandparent" item and which grandparent did it on List 1: Parent Relationship*). Those things wounded me. I forgive them, release all judgments against them, and break all unholy soul ties with them.

2. Sexual Sin - I repent of my sexual sins with the following people, and I renounce and break all unholy soul ties both with them and their sexual partners: (*name each person on List 2: Sexual Sin*), and all other sexual partners I may not recall.

3. Unforgiveness — I repent of my unforgiveness towards certain people who have hurt me. I choose now to forgive, release all judgments towards, and renounce and break all unholy soul ties with the following people: (*name each person on List 3: Unforgiveness*).

4. **Generational Sins** — I repent of the sins inherited from my mother and father, and I place those sins under your blood. I repent specifically for the sins of (*name each sin on List 4: Generational Sins*), and I cancel the assignment of every spirit upon me and my family from all generational sins, and I declare they have no hold over me.

5. **Occult** — I repent of and renounce all activity I have engaged in within the demonic realm and all other occultic activities, including: (*name each activity on List 5: Occult*). I renounce and break all unholy soul ties between those with whom I committed these sins, including (*name each person with whom you did the activity*).

6. **Word Curses** - I repent of believing word curses spoken over me. I renounce and break their power over me, and I renounce and break all unholy soul ties with those who spoke these curses about me, including the following word curses and people (*name each word curse, and who spoke them over you, on List 6: Word Curses*). I also break all unknown curses and those I have spoken over myself. I cancel the assignment of every spirit upon me from these curses and declare you have no hold over me any further.

7. **Covenants and Vows** — I repent of breaking certain covenants and vows I have made, including: (*name each broken covenant/vow on List 7: Covenants and Vows*).

8. **Idolatry** — I repent of all idolatry and placing things in my life ahead of you, Lord Jesus, including, but not limited to: (*name each item on List 8: Idolatry*).

9. **Pride** - I repent of my sin of pride, and especially the pride of (*name each item on List 9: Pride*). I also repent

that I have been prideful about my accomplishments and not giving you the glory.

10. **Abuse / Trauma** — I have had certain abusive and traumatic experiences happen to me, and I repent of my sinful responses to them. I renounce and break all unholy soul ties with those involved, including the following: (*name each event, sinful emotion or response, and individuals involved on List 10: Abuse and Trauma*). And Lord, I ask that you remove the memory of these abuses and traumas — including any from my mother and father — from my mind and my body. I rebuke all spirits tied to these abuses and traumas, and command you to leave — go now, in Jesus name!

11. **Addictions** — I repent of my sin in doing the following addictive behaviors. I renounce and break all unholy soul ties with those I did these activities with, including but not limited to: (*name each addiction and individuals you did them with on List 11: Addictions*).

12. **Other religions** — I repent of all idolatry and involvement in all other religions ("including..." *name each religion on List 12: Other Religions*).

13. **Other sins** — I also repent of the following sins (*name each sin on List 13: Other Sins*).

16. **Additional Sins and Activities** — I repent of and renounce all sins, emotions, and activities I have done, and continue to do, that are contrary to you, including: (*name each item marked on List 16: Additional Sins and Issues*). I renounce and break all unholy soul ties with each person involved that either triggered those responses or with whom I did those activities.

And now, in Jesus' name, I command every unholy spirit to leave me immediately. I declare you have no further right to torment me, and I command you to go *now*, in Jesus' name, and go where Jesus tells you to go.

> ***Instructions for next section:*** *bind each Strongman spirit on List 16: "Additional Sins and Issues" page (Strongman spirits are the headings in **ALL CAPS**), along with the junior spirits marked as being strong, consistent issues in your life; then command them out. Example: "I bind the Strongman spirit of **FEAR**, and I bind all of your kingdom to you as one, including **timidity**, **worry**, and **panic attacks**..."*

I bind the Strongman spirit of (*name one Strongman spirit from List 16: Additional Sins and Issues*), and I bind all of your kingdom to you as one, including: (*name its junior spirits marked underneath it*). And now, I declare you have no legal right to remain. In Jesus' name, I command you and all of your kingdom out right now — get out, go to Jesus, and never return! (*Repeat for every Strongman [and junior] spirit on your list*).

I also speak to every spirit of infirmity, and I command you to go as well, and take all your roots with you — remove all my sickness. _____, go! (*name each infirmity, individually, from List 15: Infirmity* — ex: "back pain, go!" Repeat for each).

In Jesus' name, I bind all unholy spirits associated with any and all curses, pacts, spells, seals, hexes, vexes, triggers, trances, vows, demonic blessings, or any other demonic bondages sent against me or my family. I bind all unholy spirits, separately and individually. I break all seals, and I command all of you to leave.

Lord Jesus, I ask that you enforce my freedom from the curse of sin for which you shed your blood and have promised to free me from. I ask that you remove all un-holy spirits from my life right now. I believe you will; and I thank you for doing so. Amen!

Prayer #2
Renounce **Agreement Sins**

Pray **3 times a day** for **3 days**. Pray **out loud.**

Since sins of iniquity committed by my forefathers may be imputed to me, and any "agreement sins" made by my forefathers, such as oaths contrary to God, are often binding upon me, I therefore speak to all sins entered into my family line, either by me or my forefathers, as my sin.

Father, I confess and believe in your Son, Jesus, as my Savior, and my loyalties are solely to you and Jesus as my Lord. I now renounce all blessings and all curses of all other religions, including: (*name each religion on List 12: Other Religions*), and of all organizations and lodges, including the Masonic lodge. I no longer want any of their benefits, nor will I be bound by any of their curses. I declare that I am under the blood of Jesus, and the power of these things was defeated by him at the cross.

I repent of and ask your forgiveness, for both me and my ancestors, including: (*name each person from List 14: Agreement Sins, and the group or sin they participated in*), for all participation in any group or activity with oaths, rituals, ceremonies or actions that are contrary to you. You alone are God, and you alone deserve my allegiance. My loyalties and allegiances are to you alone as Lord. If I, or any member of my family, have violated the first commandment by swearing allegiance to, or worshipping, a "deity" named Jahbulon* (*pronounced "Jah-bull-on"*) who is not God, or any other unholy spirit, I completely and utterly reject and renounce that worship and allegiance. Additionally, I completely and utterly reject and renounce, with the full force of my will, all oaths, allegiances, worship, covenants and participation, either made by me or any of my ancestors, with Jahbulon and all other unholy spirits, including those of other religions either I or my ancestors have participated in, such as: (*name each religion and/or spirit on List 12: Other Religions*). And by the blood of Jesus, your Son, I ask forgiveness for those oaths, allegiances, worship, covenants and participation, both for me and my family.

> ** Per internet research, Jahbulon is listed as "the true name of God" in the manual of a mainstream secret society. It is a composite of three names: Jehovah (**Jah**), Baal (**Bul**), and Osiris (**On**). Baal is an Assyrian deity that led people to human sacrifice, and Osiris is an Egyptian deity. The name Jahbulon is a perversion of the Trinity of God, and is included in certain oaths as the object of a member's loyalty and allegiance.*

I hereby break and renounce all unholy oaths and all covenants of any form taken by me and my ancestors, especially any I may have just listed above. I forever separate myself and my family from Jahbulon and all other unholy "deities" and spirits, including those of: (*name each religion and spirit on List 12: Other Religions*). On the authority of Jesus Christ, I command you, Jahbulon, and all those other spirits, to release me and each member of my family, and go! I will not serve you, any lodge, or any other religion.

If I, or anyone in my family, possess any objects associated with any unholy organization's oaths or covenants (*name any object you are aware of*), I break those oaths, covenants, and all legal rights any unholy spirit may claim with those objects. I declare those objects neutralized and ineffective, in Jesus' name. Additionally, I declare all unholy spirits tied to those objects to be severed from them, and I command each of you to leave now, in Jesus' name, and go directly and immediately to Jesus for your next assignment.

Father, I ask you to block any unholy spirits — those that may have entered my family line through my sins or those of my ancestors — from passing to my subsequent generations. If any unholy spirits entered my bloodline through my sin or those of my ancestors, I ask you to pardon the torment due to those sins and free us from those spirits. Since all of those sins are imputed to me and my family, I repent of those sins personally, and I claim the blood of Jesus, your Son, over them. I also repent for any subsequent sins from those spirits affecting anyone in my family line, and I claim your Son's blood over those sins as well.

If any unholy spirits have entered my family line because of a curse, spell, or enchantment done by others, I ask that you give me the grace to forgive those people and release all judgments against them. I forgive them for any effects caused by their sins committed against my family line, and for any damage they may have caused, and I release all judgments against them. I ask you, Lord, to break every curse, spell, or enchantment that is still in place against us.

Father, I repent of any sins that may be the result of generational spirits in my family, and I ask you to block any power those spirits may have gained in my family line because of my own sin. Please heal any damage in my life and in the lives of my family members due to those generational spirits.

I bind, and completely and utterly reject, with the full force of my will, any sin or spiritual defect of mine or any that have been imputed to me, as well as any temptation, allurements, or power that any unholy spirit may have over me as a result of my sin or the sins of any other person.

Father, I ask you to bind, in your Son Jesus' precious blood, any and all curses, pacts, spells, seals, hexes, vexes, triggers, trances, vows, demonic blessings, or any other demonic bondages sent against me or my family or any object. I ask you to bind them all and break them.

And in the name of Jesus and by his blood, I bind all unholy spirits, separately and individually, in my life and the lives of my family, including: (*name each sin and action, including its header in ALL CAPS, marked on List 16: Additional Sins and Activities*). I break all seals, curses, spells, demonic blessings, and all other demonic bondages sent against me, my family, or any object, and I command all of you spirits to leave, in Jesus' name, and never return. Leave now!

(if you or your ancestors have participated in other religions)
> I command all spirits of (*name each *religion* on List 12: Other Religions*), and specifically (*name each *spirit* on List 12: Other Religions*), to leave me and each of my family members in the name of Jesus Christ. Leave now!

I also command the spirits of Death, Infirmity, Divination and Rebellion to leave me and each of my family members, in the name of Jesus Christ. Leave now!

I also speak to every spirit of infirmity in me and each of my family members, and command you to go as well; and take all your roots and sickness with you. ____, go! (*name each infirmity, individually, on List 15: Infirmity* — ex: "back pain, go!")

I speak to all other unholy spirits, either in or around me and my family. In the authority of Jesus and by his blood, I break every remaining legal right you claim, and I command you to leave us now. Go, and never return! I speak protection over my family. I declare our properties, our persons, and our pursuits off limits to all attacks. I declare every attack of all unholy spirits upon any of us, upon our belongings, our pursuits and occupations, to be ineffective.

Father, I now ask in Jesus' name that you release your healing power into my body and the bodies of each of my family members. Fully restore everything the thief has stolen, killed, or destroyed. Please heal (*name each infirmity desired to be healed*).

I pray all of this in the Holy Name of Jesus, and through the power of God the Father, and of the Son, and of the Holy Spirit. Amen.

[**Reminder**: once you have completed the three days of Prayer #2, return to your Issue Grid and rate the intensity level of each item. Also, add any additional items you missed but are noticing changes in.]

Prayer #3
"Final Cleanup"

Pray **twice a day** (morning and evening)
for **30 days**. Pray **out loud.**
(after 30 days, using this as a daily prayer)

Before beginning, chart word curses from your Word Curses list, and beside each curse write a scripture verse that counteracts it (ex. word curse: "you'll never amount to anything" — scripture: Psalm 139:14 — "I am fearfully and wonderfully made.")

———————————

Heavenly Father, I come to you in Jesus' name, being made one with him through the new covenant in his blood. I ask for your grace to help me deny myself, die to myself, be fully led by your Spirit, and no longer conform to the patterns of this world. Help me to be closer to you, be more intimate with you, diligently pursue you, and take every thought captive through the Word of Christ.

I ask you to guide and help me to diligently pursue the work you have called me to do in service to you. And in that pursuit, guide me in increased intimacy with you, and help me to see reality through the lens of your Word rather than the lens of my eyes.

Please abundantly provide for me and my family — not only in full financial provision, but also through health in both body and relationships with each other. Prosper all that we do, and grant us the abundant life your Son has promised us.

Watch over and protect my family, and bless all of us to pursue you, to focus on you, to yield to you, to deny ourselves, and bring you glory in all we do. I repent of my sins (*list specific sins you are aware of*), I forgive each person who has hurt me, and I release all judgments against them (*list anyone that comes to mind*). And I break all unholy soul ties I have with any person. On behalf of (*spouse*), I repent of his/her sins and break all unholy soul ties he/she may have with any person, and on behalf of my children — (*name them*) — I repent for each of their sins and break all unholy soul ties they may have with any person as well. I claim Jesus' blood over all our sins, and I command all unholy spirits to leave us now! Go, in Jesus' name!

For each of my family members, I now break, by the authority of Jesus Christ, every curse put upon us. I break all curses, seals, spells, all word curses either spoken over each of us or that have been written or texted, and all other unholy bondages sent against me, my family, or any object we possess. And in the name of Jesus, I command every spirit associated with those curses to be bound, leave, and never return to us.

In the name of Jesus and through his blood, I bind and sever every cord of every unholy spirit over our home. I render every unholy spirit inactive. I declare you are cut off from your communication. I declare confusion into your camp, I declare all of your works ineffective against me and my family, and I command you out of my home in Jesus' name.

For each of my family members (*name them*), in the name of Jesus, I bind every demonic stronghold at work in our lives, including: (*list any sin strongholds the Lord places on your heart*). I bind every named and unnamed spirit under each of these stronghold spirits. I declare each spirit inactive in our lives, and I declare all their works ineffective. I break every legal right you have to remain, and I command you to leave now and never return.

(if you suffer from word curses)
>And Lord, help me renew my mind in who I am in Christ. I am (*read through each scripture verse counteracting Word Curses*)

(if you have had a long-term chronic issue)
>And Lord, I repent of my identity of (*name the chronic issue, such as "being in pain"*), and I command the spirit of (*name the chronic issue*) to leave and never return.

I ask that you enforce the freedom which you have promised from the curse of sin, and that you remove all unholy spirits from my life right now. I also ask you to release healing into my body and those of my family members. Fully restore all that the thief has stolen.

Lord, I also ask that you remove the memory of all abuses and traumas any of us have experienced — both from my mind and body, and the minds and bodies of each family member. I rebuke all spirits tied to those abuses and traumas, and I command each of you to leave — go now in Jesus' name!

And Lord, I ask you to strengthen my memory, cognitive ability, thinking power, and imagination. Help me, also, to remember those things I should remember, and not remember those things I should forget.

Please bring forth the fruit of your Spirit each day, in me and each member of my family — love, joy, peace, patience, goodness, gentleness, faithfulness, and self-control. Grant us mercy in all we do, and help us to lean on you each day.

I pray this all in the name of the Father, and of the Son, and of the Holy Spirit. Amen!

[**Reminder**: once you have completed the thirty days of Prayer #3, return to your Issue Grid and rate the intensity level of each item. Also, add any additional items you missed but are noticing changes in.]

Chapter 13

Helping others by "giving it forward"

H opefully by this time, if you've been praying the Prayer of Freedom, you're seeing a lot of issues melt away from your life. If you are, it's because you're repenting of sins and the Lord is removing spirits of discipline from you.

So, now that you're getting free, let's talk about helping set others free, too...

Give it forward — helping family and others get free themselves

As I mentioned earlier, if your spouse or children struggle with issues, I suggest giving each of them their own copy of *The Prayer of Freedom* so they can read it themselves, do their own worksheets, and pray through the prayers personally.

Additionally, if you have extended family or friends struggling with issues, give them a copy, too. As it has with you, it will help them understand what's happening and how to get free. I have found that *giving* **them a book is more effective than telling them to buy it**. If you *tell* them to buy it, most get busy and don't. But if you *give* it to them, 100% of them will receive it. And many (if not all) will ultimately read and act on it, *especially* if you use the simple technique I'll share in just a moment.

I remember years back a book by Bruce Wilkinson made a tremendous impact on my life with several things I was going through at the time. It was so impactful that I ended up buying cases worth of books and giving them out to friends, clients and people I met (I literally bought those books in groups of 50). I didn't know the term "give it forward" at the time, but that's exactly what I was doing.

And if you've seen the Prayer of Freedom work in *your* life and feel led, as I am, to set God's people free, then let me suggest you do the same with this book, too...

Buy and keep a handful of *The Prayer of Freedom* books to share with others. I do this myself, and I am *deliberate* about giving them out.

Wherever I go, I carry a copy — going out to lunch, running an errand, or anything else. Before I go, I ask the Lord, "Please lead me to someone you want to set free so I can give them this book." And he usually does! It's a great way to minister to others.

So, I challenge you to do the same thing. Carry a copy wherever you go for times when the Lord puts someone in your path who could use it (a co-worker, friend, or random person you meet). Make it a personal ministry of yours — keep several in your car, at the house, and even in your purse or bag so you always have one to give to someone in need.

And if you are tight on money, don't let that hold you back. Here's why...

The Lord directs us to honor him with tithes and offerings. When we give to the Lord by giving to various organizations, our money is ultimately used to help God's children. Some of our giving may pay a preacher's salary to teach God's word. Some may support missionaries who share the Gospel. And some may pay for counseling, food pantries, or other outreach ministries.

In other words, when we give to the Lord, our money is ultimately *paying* for things to help his children.

Because of that, if money is tight but you desire to keep a supply of books on hand to share with others, here's a suggestion...

All the money you give to the Lord, regardless of *where* you give it, is his. If you give to a church, it's the Lord's money. If you give to a mission organization, it's the Lord's money. And if you buy a poor person's groceries, it's still the Lord's money.

Because it's all the Lord's money, ask the Lord if he wants you to take part of *his* money to purchase extra copies of *The Prayer of Freedom* to give away as your own ministry outreach.

Years ago, I asked the Lord the same question — did he want me to take part of *his* money and spend it directly on his children when they were in need? I felt strongly that he was directing me to do that, so I did.

And it has been the most freeing experience I've ever had. Why? Because I'm no longer spending *my* money, I'm spending *his*. And because it's his, I don't hesitate to be generous when someone is in need.

This is what Jesus meant in **Matthew 25:40** (paraphrased) when he said: "Whatever you do for the least of my children, you do for me." In other words, when I buy a grocery cart of food for a young mother of three who is struggling financially, I don't hesitate. I'm spending the Lord's money, not mine. I'm doing it for him.

So, if money is tight, go on and ask the Lord about using part of his money you're already giving him to buy extra copies of *The Prayer of Freedom*. If he says, "Yes," then freely buy as many as you want to keep on hand. It's no longer coming from your family budget, but from what you're already giving him, anyway.

Ultimately, the Lord's #1 desire is for his children to repent and return to him. And there are few things more effective in accomplishing that than giving them a copy of this book that will make them *want* to repent!

That's why I'm so passionate about encouraging you to share *The Prayer of Freedom* with others. There is a second reason that is even *more* important, but I'll share that later in Chapter 15, so be sure to read it.

If you want extra copies of this book to keep on hand, you can buy them at any bookstore, by scanning the QR code on the cover of this book, or use this link: www.**ThePrayerOfFreedom*Book*.com** (at the time of this writing, we are also working on creating discounted options for 10 or more books at this link).

An easy way to get people *wanting* the book — the "3 Questions Approach"

If you plan to give away this book to others, here's the most effective way I've found to do it.

First, I always keep several books in my car so I can grab one as I exit.

Next, I deliberately look for opportunities to start conversations with people. It's often a server at a restaurant, someone in line for the checkout counter, or anyone else.

Once we're talking, I ask them three key questions. I call this the "3 Questions Approach," and it's *these* questions that make this process work. Here it is...

▶ *3 Questions Approach* ◀

Question #1: "Can I ask you a strange question?"

Question #2: "Do you ever feel like you're carrying a heavy backpack through life, and every day it keeps getting heavier... or do you ever struggle with things like anxiety or depression?"

Question #3: "Would you like to get rid of it?"

That's it! I have found when I ask these questions, most people say "yes" to all of them. When they do, I offer them the book.

If you use this approach, you'll be surprised at how easy it is and how many people want to be set free. You can even use it when talking to people on the phone. It's not as effective as *giving* them a book in person, but it's the next best thing. Here's how I do it...

Whenever I'm talking with someone — like a friend or customer service rep at a company — and we're wrapping up our call, I'll ask Question #1:

"Before I let you go, could I ask you a strange question?"

They usually say, "sure!" Then I ask Question #2:

"Do you ever feel like you're carrying a heavy backpack through life and it keeps getting heavier every day — or do you ever struggle with things like anxiety or depression?"

Most say "yes." Then I follow up with Question #3:

"Would you like to get rid of it?"

They *always* say "yes," and I share about the book...

"I've read a book that has a *90% success rate* in

helping people get rid of these things. Let me give you a link to learn more about it. When you go there, just read the description of the book, and if you like it, get it. Here's the link..." (then I speak it out slowly) **"The Prayer Of Freedom *Book* .com."**

Let me share how easy this works...

Today, as I'm writing this, I had to handle a couple of issues with my internet service. In the process I've spoken with five customer service reps. I used the "3 Questions Approach" with each of them, and all five said "yes" to every question. Then, when I shared about the book, they all wanted to write down the link and check it out... and *four* of them were so hungry for it they sincerely thanked me for sharing it!

This "3 Questions Approach" is *so* easy to use. And all it takes is to *deliberately* start conversations with people so you can ask them the questions. And whether you use it in person or by phone, you'll be surprised with how many people are hurting, and how easily you can help set them free. It will truly warm your heart!

How to ensure people read the book when you give it to them in person

How many times has someone given you a book that you intended to read, but got too busy and it ultimately ended up on a bookshelf somewhere?

I hate to admit it, but I probably have one or two bookshelves *full* of books just like that — books I intended to read, but never started!

When you give a copy of this book to someone, it won't help them unless they read it. So, here's a simple technique that is extremely effective.

The key is to get them to *start* reading the book. If they read the "About This Book" section, it will likely grab their attention and make them want to read the entire book. Here's how I do it — I ask them what I call the "Commitment Question."

When I hand the book to someone, I open it to the "About This Book" section and show them how short it is (only about 3 pages). Then I ask them the "Commitment Question"...

▶ *Commitment Question* ◀

"I will give this to you under *one* condition — that you promise to read this section, "About This Book," *before* you go to bed tonight. It takes three minutes for the average person. Will you commit to that?"

If they say, "Yes," then I give them the book.

That's it! If they will verbally commit to reading that section, the vast majority will honor their commitment. When they do, most will get interested and start reading the entire book, and eventually do the prayer.

Another way to help set people free is to share how this prayer has impacted your life on social media. Post it on Facebook, Instagram, and whatever other social media apps you use. The more others hear about it and read it, the more lives you will impact.

Chapter 14

Staying free... and praying to set family members free, too

Now, let's talk about how to stay free yourself, and how to pray and repent on family members' behalf to set them free as well.

Finalizing getting free yourself

If you have completed Prayer #3 for its 30 days and some issues still remain, don't be concerned. It sometimes happens that way, and all it means is those issues may take a little longer to go away.

If this happens, here are a few simple steps to do...

First, mark their intensity levels on your issue grid and see how much they've reduced already. Then, go back and repeat Prayer #2 and Prayer #3. Once you finish them, re-grade the intensity levels of those issues. If they are diminishing, then keep repeating this process until they completely disappear.

If they remain the same (or increase) from one month to the other, it usually means a spirit of discipline still has a legal right to you. If this happens, go back through the List Preparation Guide and ask the Lord to reveal any sins you may have missed, then list out any *additional* sins he brings to mind.

Write down *anything* you feel he is sharing, no matter how small or absurd you think it may be. If you're wrong, it won't hurt to repent of it. If you're right, it could set you free.

If, after doing this process, you continue to struggle with things you feel have a spiritual root, I recommend seeking help from a trained, Christian professional.

While the Prayer of Freedom is effective in many areas, there are things in the spirit realm it may not directly address, and getting help from a trained professional can make all the difference.

To find the right person, ask the Lord to direct you where to go. Then, search online for Christian counseling groups that specialize in "deliverance" ministry. You will likely find a number of groups that can help.

Staying free *personally*

Now that you know how God's discipline works, the easiest way to stay free is to (1) **stop sinning** and (2) **repent quickly** if you do sin. Here are seven suggestions to help...

First (this is *very* important), keep praying the morning and evening prayer (Prayer #3) as an ongoing, daily prayer, even after the thirty days have passed. It covers all the basics to keep spirits of discipline from returning again.

Second (this is also *very* important), monitor yourself. If you start slipping back into the challenges you had before doing the prayer, it means you became lax with repentance and invited spirits of discipline to return. This often happens when there are ongoing relationship issues that create unforgiveness and bitterness, addiction problems where you feel strong enough to "take another drink" (or whatever the urge) and you fall back into your old habits, and things of that sort. If you start slipping back, simply *repeat* the entire Prayer of Freedom process, starting with making a list of *new* sins you haven't repented of since the last time you did the prayer. If you do this, along with praying Prayer #3 daily, you'll stay free the rest of your life.

Third, the most important way to sin less is to spend more time with God. Spend time reading the Bible, praying, and praising him on a daily basis. Whatever time you've normally been spending on these things (if any), set a plan to increase it by 50%. Then, once you do, increase it again. The more time you spend with the Lord on a one-on-one basis, the more his Spirit operates through you, and the less you give into sinful temptations.

Fourth, set boundaries in your life where you know you are weak and are more likely to give into temptation. Satan knows your weaknesses and purposely tries to get you into positions where you are weak. Once you're there, you're more likely to give into temptations to sin. That's his strategy, by the way. If he can get you to sin while you're weak, then you hand over legal rights for spirits of discipline to come in and attack.

To set those boundaries, take the issues you've struggled with — maybe it's pornography, or drinking, or "blowing your top" and yelling at a loved one — and analyze when you typically do those things. You'll start to see patterns as to when those sins occur.

For example, if you struggle with pornography, you may find you usually do it late at night when you're tired. Or if you struggle with drinking, it may be after a hard day's work and you just want to relax with a drink, or it may be when you're around certain friends. Or if it's "flipping out" in anger, it may be either when certain trigger-words are said or they are said in a particular manner.

Once you find the patterns of when you are most likely to do those sins, simply place boundaries in your life to keep yourself from being in those situations.

Fifth, ask the Lord to direct you on things to stop doing that may be influencing you in ways that cause you to sin. This could be anything from the friends you hang out with, the books or movies you consume, or the music you listen to. Everything you allow into your life will influence you in one way or another. And those things that influence you will, ultimately, influence the things you do.

Sixth, if you possess any objects tied to a group or organization known for agreement sins or the occult, get rid of those objects. This could be any sort of object — clothing, swords, shields, trinkets, coins, or anything similar that may be tied to a secret society, a spirit guide, or any sort of witchcraft, or occult group. Oftentimes, spirits of discipline are tied to those objects, and if you hold onto them you give those spirits legal rights to you.

To get rid of them, don't simply sell them or give them away because you'll just be passing legal rights to someone else.

I remember a friend of mine and his teenage son were given a painting by a customer of theirs. It was a weird, mystical looking painting, but they thought nothing of it and received the gift with gratitude. However, almost immediately the father and son began arguing a lot and started growing apart, and within a few months they were completely estranged from each other. The son would have nothing to do with him — he wouldn't talk to him, spend time with him, or even acknowledge his existence. It was as if, for some inexplicable reason, the son hated his father.

Also, simultaneously during this time, the son went spiraling downward into a deep, dark mental abyss. He started getting involved in all kinds of terrible activities, doing things he knew were horribly wrong, but he couldn't stop himself.

Then, a year later, the father was prompted to burn the painting. And as soon as he did, *everything* lifted off of his son and all the mental torment left. The father-son relationship immediately began to restore. It was the difference between night and day.

What happened was there was a legal right tied to that painting, and that legal right gave an unholy spirit — a spirit of discipline — the right to attack the owner. As soon as it was burned, the legal rights were removed and the spirit left.

This is why it's so important to get rid of *anything* that could be tied to an organization or group or activity that is involved with agreement sins or the occult.

And while it may seem a bit extreme, believe it or not, the best thing to do if you have any of those objects is to break them into pieces, burn them in a fire, then scatter the remains far away from you.

Seventh, if someone has suffered with a chronic issue for many years — maybe some form of nagging pain — and it goes away after praying the Prayer of Freedom, I have witnessed occasions where the pain returns. It's as if the spirit of discipline that originally caused the pain came back. Here's why it may do that, and what you can do so it doesn't happen to you...

As strange as it may sound, when people have had prolonged issues for years that the Lord brings freedom to, they often feel "awkward" without that issue.

For example, "Tim" may have had excruciating hip pain for fifteen years. Now that it's gone, it just doesn't feel "normal" anymore.

What's going on is, over the years, he had become so accustomed to it that he built up an "identity" of being in pain. So, once that pain disappeared, he may have unconsciously thought in his heart, "This doesn't feel right. I should still be in pain." And because that identity is contrary to God's identity for him — which makes it a sin — the spirit of discipline has a legal right to return and keep Tim in pain.

How does Tim keep this from happening? By simply repenting of his "identity" of being in pain.

You'll see this in Prayer #3 where, if you've dealt with a chronic issue in your life, you repent of any identity you still have with that issue. Thankfully, you don't have to do this forever — just long enough to re-train your identity until you no longer have that issue.

Helping children with behavior problems

If you have young children with behavior problems — maybe they're overly antsy and can't sit still, maybe they've been diagnosed with ADHD, maybe they're always rebellious or angry — sometimes these could be tied to spirits of discipline. Try praying the Prayer of Freedom on their behalf, or guide them through praying a simple, child-level version of it themselves.

As I shared earlier in the "About This Book" section, I did this with a friend of mine who had a young, eight year old girl. She was overly active to the point of being extreme, and it was wearing him and his wife out. So, one night while we were visiting in the living room, I guided him through a simple version of the Prayer of Freedom for his daughter.

He came up to me the next day, astounded. He said, "My daughter is completely different! She is still an active, eight year old girl, but she is *calm*. All of the 'high-voltage' type of hyper fidgetiness is gone!"

Helping family members get free by repenting on their behalf

The most effective person to repent of sins is the one who committed them. However, in God's grace, he often allows us to repent for the sins of others when we have authority over them (ex. our children, either biological or adopted), when we are in covenant with them (ex. our spouse), and even close loved ones (ex. our parents).

This ability to repent on behalf of someone else's sins is based on "authority." If you have spiritual authority, you can repent of their sins as it relates to freeing them from spirits of discipline. I am *not* suggesting you can repent of someone else's sins as it relates to their salvation, but I've seen this authority in action multiple times as it relates to helping a loved one get free from unholy spirits.

I'll give you Biblical evidence in a moment but, suffice it to say, because of this authority you can repent on behalf of your children, on behalf of your spouse, and possibly even other loved ones to help break discipline from their lives.

If your spouse or child has the ability and willingness to do the Prayer of Freedom on his or her own, that's always most effective. But if they can't or won't, your authority as a parent or spouse can go a long way to help.

As a side note, even if they *do* pray it for themselves, if you pray with them and *on their behalf* at the same time, it can have a dramatic impact. Many of the stories I've shared throughout this book were occasions when I prayed *with* the individual and interceded on their behalf at the same time they were praying. When I did, it wasn't unusual to see *all* their issues disappear immediately. While I do believe they would have received similar results if they had prayed only on their own, it likely would have taken a few days, to as long as a month or more, to see the same results.

If you recall the stories I shared of Dennis, the elderly father who repented on behalf of his adult son who could never recover financially; or the story of Kate, who repented on her husband's behalf when he went into anaphylactic shock; or the story of Richard, who repented on behalf of his son who had gone into a deep depression for two years after a terrible divorce — in all of these cases it was their spiritual authority that allowed them to repent on the other person's behalf.

This authority is one of the mysteries of God's spiritual laws. It makes no sense using man's wisdom; but the real life applications I've seen show these laws clearly allow for it, and God honors it.

Where do you find these laws of authority in the Bible?

Once you're aware of what to look for, you'll see them throughout. Let me show you three of them now...

The first is **Numbers 30:3** where it describes the authority a man has over both his virgin daughter and his wife. In both cases, if either of them enter a legally binding contract without his knowledge, once he finds out about it he can break the contract and remove all legal rights against his daughter or wife. This authority can also be applied to repenting (breaking) the legal rights of sin, and is available to both the father and mother for a child.

The second is in **Job 1:5.** You have to read the full chapter to catch the significance of it, but this passage describes how Job would offer sacrifices to the Lord (our modern-day equivalent of repentance) on behalf of his children "in case they sinned against the Lord.'"

And we see the impact of this with Satan. In the interaction between God and Satan, Satan (called the "accuser of the brethren" because he accuses them of sin) is upset at God for placing a hedge of protection around Job, thereby, not allowing Satan to attack him.

Satan's only power comes from his ability to accuse people of sin. Once they are accused, he has a legal right to attack. But he was prevented from accusing Job and his family. Why? Because Job was righteous (no sin to accuse him of) and constantly sacrificed (repented) for his children's sins. And we can infer that, since he consistently did it on their behalf, he did it on his own behalf as well.

What you see in this passage with Job is a father repenting on behalf of his children, and God honoring that repentance by blocking Satan's ability to attack. That's what a "hedge of protection" is — it's the blocking of unholy spirits from attacking you, and it happens when there are no unrepented sins for which they can attack.

The third passage is from **Genesis 2:24.** This is where God declares that a man and woman shall come together as husband and wife, and the two will become one flesh. This is talking about the marriage covenant, which makes two people one in God's eyes.

We see this mystery with the eternal covenant between the Father and Jesus (cf. **Hebrews 13:20**). In **John 14:9**, Jesus says he and the Father are one when he says, "Whoever has seen me has seen the Father." (ESV)

How can two persons be one? It's because of the covenant. That's what covenants do — they make two persons operate as one.

In a similar way, husband and wife are one because of their marriage covenant. And since the two are one, one spouse can repent for the sins committed by the other. This is what Kate did when her husband went into anaphylactic shock.

I don't know how far this authority extends. Are there *some* sins you can't repent of on behalf of a child or spouse or another loved one? I'm not sure.

What I do know, however, is I've seen this authority in action, and I've seen it bring relief to others. I understand the truth of its existence; I just don't know the extent to how far you can take it.

I do have a simple rule-of-thumb to offer, though.

If there is a child, spouse or another loved one you want to pray the Prayer of Freedom for on their behalf, and you repent for sins you *don't* have authority to repent of, the only thing that will happen is... are you ready for this? ... *nothing.* That's it!

There are *no* repercussions for repenting. If you don't have the authority, nothing will happen. But if you do have the authority, God will honor it and set them free!

Therefore, my simple rule-of-thumb on this is, *try it.* If you're wrong, it won't hurt. But if you're right, it might set them free!

‣ How to pray on someone else's behalf

If you want to pray this prayer on someone else's behalf, all you have to do is slightly adjust the process.

First, when you do the List Preparation Guide, do it as if *you* are the person you are praying for. In other words, if you are praying for "Tom," then create the lists as if *you* were Tom. Make a list of *his* sins that you know about. Don't worry if you don't know all the sins he may have done. Ask the Lord for guidance on what to include, then trust the Lord to reveal what you need to write down. When in doubt, write down *whatever* comes to mind, even if it seems absurd. If you're wrong, it won't hurt to repent of it. If you're right, it might set him free.

Second, when you do the prayers, re-word them to apply to the person as you read them. For example, if you are praying for Tom and the prayer says, "I repent of unforgiveness towards the following people," simply pray "I repent *on Tom's behalf* for *his* unforgiveness towards the following people."

And **third**, if you are praying on behalf of a child (even an adult child), it's best for both mother and father to do the Prayer of Freedom *first* **before praying for the child**. There may be agreement sins being passed down to the child from one or both sides that should be renounced before praying for the child. However, if the other parent isn't willing or able to pray, then, when you pray on your child's behalf, be sure to renounce any agreements sins you know of that may be coming down through the other parent's lineage. You may also want to complete the following sections of the List Preparation Guide on behalf of the other parent and repent of those sins as you pray for your child: **List 4** Generational Sins, **List 5** Occult, **List 8** Idolatry, **List 12** Other Religions, and **List 14** Agreement Sins.

Chapter 15

The REAL reason I wrote this book... it *will* surprise you

Now that you understand the *power* of repentance, I want to share the REAL reason I wrote this book. Why? Because I want to *recruit* you to help me with it.

Besides the Lord directing me to write it, there are two personal reasons I wrote this book. The *second* one will surprise you! I'll share them now because this is what I want you to help me with...

The first reason I wrote this book is to set people free. I've seen so much heartache and so many challenges literally melt away in people's lives after they repent of their sins that I have to tell the world about it! I want people set free so they can pursue their God-given destiny with zeal. I want to see them further God's kingdom here on earth and fulfill the destiny he has for their lives — the "good works he prepared beforehand" that Paul talks about in **Ephesians 2:10**.

So, if you've found this book helpful, please help set others free by sharing it with them. Keep a few books on hand and "give it forward" when the Lord places someone in your path who needs help.

The second reason — and this is the one I really want to "recruit" you to help with — will surprise you. It's a **bold, *audacious* goal**...

I want to set *nations* free, and I need your help.
Together, I believe we can do it.

I live in the United States of America where we face many challenges with plenty of issues going on. I believe the root cause of most of them is the sins we, as a nation, have been committing against the Lord for generations. And if you live in any other nation, I'm certain you can say the same about your nation, too.

The Lord called me in late 2020 to repent daily on behalf of my nation. I asked him, "What do I repent for?" He directed me to the Ten Commandments. The Ten Commandments are God's standard of holiness — that's why they are so holy. Ultimately, most sins are either a transgression against or perversion of one of these Ten Commandments.

The bottom line is, God brings judgment against nations because of their sins. And he relents of that judgment if the people repent.

The book of Jonah talks about a wicked city named Nineveh that had been so sinful for so long that God had decreed destruction against it. God told Jonah to go preach to the Ninevites that, unless they repent, God would bring his wrath against them.

Jonah didn't want to tell them that. Nineveh was one of the archenemies of the Jewish nation. Jonah *wanted* God to destroy them. But God was merciful and wanted to relent. So, ultimately, God got his way, and Jonah preached a message of repentance. The city of Nineveh repented, and God withdrew his hand of judgment against it.

And now that you understand the amazing power of repentance, imagine what would happen if people in your nation began repenting on behalf of your nation, both for their sins and those of their fathers and mothers of past generations. If God spared Nineveh because they repented, and if God would have spared Sodom and Gomorrah if he found only a handful of righteous people there (**Genesis 18:28-32**), what would God do in *your* nation if his people would simply repent!

Here's what he promises in **2 Chronicles 7:14** (ESV): "If my people who are called by my name will humble themselves, and pray and seek my face, and turn from their wicked ways, then I will hear from heaven and will forgive their sins and heal their land."

There is still time. We can turn nations around!

In **Isaiah 46:12-13**, God is speaking to Jerusalem just "moments" before the city is destroyed, the temple is torn down, and those still alive are sent into exile to Babylon. Times are urgent and in severe crisis. But notice what God says...

"Listen to me, you stubborn people who are so far from doing right. For I am ready to set things right, not in the distant future, but right now! I am ready to save Jerusalem and show my glory to Israel." (NLT, emphasis added)

God is telling them, "There is still time. All is not lost. Repent, and I can save you right now!"

Just as we have spiritual authority to repent on behalf of a child or spouse, that authority also extends to our own nation. You can see Biblical evidence of this in Ezra 9, Nehemiah 9, and Daniel 9. In each of these passages, men repented on behalf of their nation and for the sins their forefathers had committed.

So, what do I want you to do? I want you to join me. I want you to **repent on behalf of *your* nation**... and **build an army of others to do the same.**

How do you build that army? By promoting and sharing *The Prayer of Freedom* book with as many people as you can. Give it to friends and family, share it on social media, tell others what it's done for you, get on podcast and radio interviews to tell your story. Then, start repenting on behalf of your nation, and trust the Lord to prompt the "army" you build to do the same.

Together, if we all work at this, we can turn nations around!

Below is the prayer the Lord gave me. I pray it daily. Please join me in praying it daily yourself. And please also pray the intercessory prayer following it every day for God to set his people free, too.

▸ Repentance prayer on behalf of your nation

Lord, I come to you on behalf of my nation, ____. I bring repentance to you for our sins against you. I repent that we have turned away from you as a nation and sought other gods. I repent that we worship idols our hands have made. I repent that we take your name in vain. I repent that we profane your Sabbaths. I repent that we dishonor our fathers and mothers. I repent that we commit murder, and even sacrifice our own children to Molech through abortion. I repent that we commit adultery. I repent that we steal. I repent that we bear false witness against our neighbor. I repent that we covet what our neighbor has. I repent that we commit sexual immorality, and that we pervert and twist all of your holy standards. And I place these sins under the blood of your Son, Jesus, and claim his blood over them. Please, most Holy and merciful Father, have mercy upon us and our nation. Please grant our people the grace of your repentance (*2 Timothy 2:25*) that they may repent of their wicked ways and turn towards you, so you will relent and withdraw your hand against our nation. I ask this in Jesus' name. Amen.

▸ Intercessory prayer to set God's people free

And Lord, I also ask that you set your people free through *The Prayer of Freedom* book. Please expand its distribution to get it into the hands of your people around the world. And as you do, I ask that you open their hearts and minds when they read it, that its message will bring them to repentance so you can set them free, and that they will repent daily on behalf of their own nation so you can set their nation free as well. Please also block every enemy attack that tries to thwart or "cancel" its printing and distribution. Amen.

The simple way to build an "army"

Please get the word out to help build an army to set God's people free. Here are several ways to do it...

❏ **Social Media:** share on Facebook, Instagram, and other social media platforms. Since other books have similar titles and people may get confused as to which one to buy, please link them *directly* to this book to minimize confusion and make it easier for them to learn more. For simplicity's sake, use our link if desired: www.**ThePrayerOfFreedom*Book*.com**.

❏ **Email:** email friends and family. Share your story and encourage them to get the book. Please link directly to the book to minimize any confusion as to which one to get. For simplicity's sake, use our link if desired: www.**ThePrayerOfFreedom*Book*.com**.

❏ **Keep extra copies on hand:** buy and keep extra copies of this book on hand to give to others. Make this a personal outreach ministry of yours.

❏ **Drop off copies to specific friends** you feel need it and could benefit from it.

❑ **Take a copy wherever you go** and ask the Lord to lead you to people he wants to set free, then use the "3 Questions Approach" to engage them.

❑ **Rate and review** *The Prayer of Freedom* book and share how it has impacted you so others will be encouraged to read it. Rate it on the site where you bought it, or rate it on Amazon if it was given to you.

Thank you for helping set people free!

Sample Email / Social Media message

If you aren't sure what to say in a social media or email message, here's a sample message you can use:

Have you read *The Prayer of Freedom* book?

I just read it and it was *very* impactful! I encourage you to get a copy.

It shares a special approach to prayer with an almost 90% success rate in helping others get rid of issues like anxiety, depression, addictions, chronic pain, traumas, and other health problems.

Here's what it did for me — [*share your story*].

If you or a loved one suffers with these types of issues, please check it out. Here's a link to where you can read the book's description to learn more or get it if desired:

www.**ThePrayerOfFreedom*Book*.com**

About our book link

Our book link (ThePrayerOfFreedom*Book*.com) has been put together for several reasons.

First, to simplify the ordering process by linking people to the correct page on various book websites for their country (for example, Amazon has different websites for different countries, and this link will automatically direct them to the correct ordering page for *their* country).

Second, to provide discounted pricing on quantities of 10 or more books, making the "give it forward" process more economical (being worked on at the time of this writing).

And **third**, to provide a central ordering location in case our current printing or distribution channels attempt to "cancel" this book.

Want more great teaching from Beatty Carmichael?

I do extensive, in-depth teaching on many Biblical topics. Please plug in and learn more. Here's how…

1. Visit my website or podcast channel: Get free access to all my teaching from my podcast channel *Get Radical Faith* or my website *GetRadicalFaith.com*

2. Subscribe to my X feed (formerly Twitter): Get periodic "nuggets" from specific Bible verses — *@GetRadicalFaith*

3. Get other books I have written: To find other books I have written, search any online bookstore for my name, *"Beatty Carmichael,"* or visit my teaching website mentioned above

4. Learn more about spiritual warfare: If you want more training on this book's topic, view my extensive teaching at GetRadicalFaith.com/SpiritualWarfare.

Appendix

List Preparation Guide

(list unrepented sins by category)

The Prayer of Freedom is most effective when you pray it for yourself. However, if you are concerned about a child or spouse who is unable (or unwilling) to do the prayer themselves, spiritual rules of authority may allow you to pray it for them, on their behalf (see Chapter 14 for details). If you do the Prayer of Freedom on their behalf, then when you do the List Preparation Guide, do it focused on them and not on yourself.

▸ **Prayer *before* making your lists**

"Lord, I ask you to remind me of every sin and person I need to include on my lists to be set free. And in Jesus' name, I bind every unholy spirit and command you *down*. And during the entire time I am making my lists and doing the prayers, I forbid any of you, in Jesus's name, to manifest, distract, confuse, or in any other way attempt to prevent me from doing either."

▸ **Prayer *each* time you complete your list for each category**

"Lord, I have now completed this list in full. If there is anything or anyone else I need to add, please bring it to my mind now."

(then wait two or three minutes. If the Lord brings something (or someone) to your attention, add it to your list. Before moving on to the next category, repeat this

process until he brings nothing more to mind. This is a crucial step to get the best results, so don't rush it.)

Create your lists in the spaces provided in this book. If you run out of space, use the blank pages at the end as "overflow" pages. If you overflow to them, be sure to **number and label your lists** with the same number and headings as below. The Prayer of Freedom references different lists to pray through at different times, so having your lists numbered and labeled properly will make it much easier to do.

If you are ready, then grab a pen and work on each list consecutively before moving on to the next one. Once you are finished with all your lists, **return to Chapter 12** and start praying through the Prayer of Freedom. And may the Lord greatly bless you!

#1 Parent Relationship

Our early childhood experiences dramatically shape our life as we grow up. For example, if a parent or grandparent abused or abandoned you as a child, it feels as if *God* abused or abandoned you. This can lead to bitterness towards God. Even if you had a "great" childhood but had to assume adult responsibilities due to a parent's absence — whether through abandonment, divorce, death, military deployment, or chronic illness — this, too, can impact your impression of God. Both parental actions and life circumstances can unconsciously create wounds that foster unforgiveness towards parents, paving the way for considerable torment in life.

Action List: create a separate list for *each* parent (one for father, one for mother, and one for grandparent). List all issues, events, traumas, abuse, rejection or actions in your life that involved you, either directly or indirectly. These could include: "abandonment due to prolonged illness" (where you had to shoulder their responsibilities), "arguments and alcohol drinking," or any negative actions that led you to make internal vows against being like them (ex. "I will not drink like my mother"), and so on. To help identify all issues, think through each age group of childhood separately — (1) less than 5 years old, (2) between 5 and 7 years old, (3) between 8 and 13 years old, (4) above 13 years old — and list all things that come to mind.

Father: _____

_____

_____

_____

_____

_____

_____

Mother: _____

_____

_____

_____

_____

_____

_____

Grandparent: _____

_____

_____

_____

_____

#2 Sexual Sin

Sexual sin is *any* sexual act you do outside of marriage.

Action List: make a list of everyone you have engaged in sexual activity with outside of marriage — including if you had sex with your spouse before you got married. If you do not remember their name, simply write a brief description (ex. "the guy with the blue hat" or "the girl at the pool party").

_____

_____

_____

_____

_____

_____

#3 Unforgiveness

Unforgiveness often leads to significant torment in people's lives. Forgiveness is a deliberate choice rather than an emotion. It involves *choosing* to forgive some-one who has harmed you. Forgiveness does *not* require you to reconcile with that person or allow that person back into your life. It is a one-sided action that *you* do. Forgiveness does not mean you agree with what that person did to you. It merely means you release your judgment against that person and free them from your heart.

Action List: make a list of everyone who has hurt you — either directly against you, or indirectly against a loved one — whether they are still living or dead (include <u>yourself</u> if you have unforgiveness toward your-self), then list every hurt they did to you.

_____

_____

_____

_____

_____

_____

#4 Generational Sins

In the Old Testament, God states he will visit the iniq-uities of the father (and mother) upon the third and fourth generations. Iniquities are grave sins that are passed down through the bloodline, meaning you in-herit them from your parents. They act as an open door for tormenting spirits to attack you. This is commonly referred to as a "generational curse." Generational curses manifest as recurring patterns of sins, illnesses, or abhorrent behaviors coming down through your ancestral lineage. Examples include **abuse, addiction, adultery, divorce, anxiety, premature death, cancer,** and more. Ancestral involvement in practices like **witchcraft, secret societies, or slavery** within one's ancestry often creates generational sins.

Action List: make a list of every pattern sin, sickness or abhorrent behavior you see in your ancestry.

_____

_____

_____

_____

_____

#5 Occult

Engaging in occultic activities can give tormenting spirits a legal right to your life. Occultic activities include: **Ouija boards, séances, hypnosis, horoscope, water divining, new age, superstition, witchcraft, Santeria, palm reading, roots or tea leaves, new age healing, astrology, numerology, tarot card readings, ancestor worship, burning sage, using crystals, levitation, spirit guides, divination, Wicca/white magic, mediums, yoga*,** any **occult-based games** (such as **Dungeons and Dragons, Magic the Gathering, Pokémon**), **martial arts religious teaching,** even **Harry Potter books** (glorifies witchcraft), etc. Another form of occultic activity is giving **praise and honor to Satan** (for example, singing along to Satanic-based songs). All of these can be open doors to be tormented.

* Yoga originates from Hinduism. There are mysteries in the spiritual realm that can open doorways into the occultic realm, and should be avoided. The danger with yoga is the positions and meditations can open the wrong doors and create legal rights against you.

Action List: make a list of (1) every type of occultic activity you have participated in, *even* if you only did it one time for just a minute or two, and (2) every person directly involved with you in those activities (those who encouraged you in the activity and who participated with you; if you don't remember their names, identify with a description such as "guy in the blue hat")

_____

_____

_____

_____

#6 Word Curses

Word curses are haunting statements spoken over you, such as "You'll never succeed," "You'll always be an addict," or "You'll never have a fulfilling relationship." These are statements spoken about you that have either come true, or you fear will come true. They can be spoken about you by others, or even by yourself. Once you *believe* a word curse, you give agreement to it. And that gives a tormenting spirit the legal right to fulfill that agreement.

Action List: make a list of every word curse spoken over you, and who spoke them to you.

_____

_____

_____

_____

#7 Covenants and Vows

Covenants and vows are commitments you make to others. If you break a covenant or vow, it may allow a spirit of torment into your life.

Action List: make a list of all covenants/vows you have broken (ex: bankruptcy, foreclosure, vows to God, etc).

_____

_____

_____

#8 Idolatry

Idolatry occurs when something takes priority over God in your life. It often involves placing excessive importance on certain things, like obsessing over your child's sport or being consumed by greed or envy. Participating in saint worship or engaging in other religions that involve offering substances at altars, shrines, or holy sites are additional forms of idolatry.

Action List: make a list of all possible forms of idolatry you have committed *at any time* in your life (ex: spouse, home, job/position, money, greed, covetousness, children, other religions, etc). Ask the Lord to reveal what, if any, actions you have done in the past which may be considered idolatry.

_____

_____

_____

_____

#9 Pride

Pride is the feeling of superiority and haughtiness when you believe yourself to be better than others in a particular aspect or area.

Action List: make a list of all things for which you are prideful (ex: if you feel you have a better marriage than others, a better ministry, a better profession, know more Bible than others).

_____

_____

_____

#10 Abuse and Trauma

Experiencing abuse, rape, abortion, a car accident, or any other traumatic event can potentially create openings for tormenting spirits. Abuse, for instance, can lead to emotional wounds (unforgiveness) and unhealthy soul ties with the abuser. Abortion can generate unholy soul ties with the aborted baby, the abortion doctor, and those who influenced you to abort your child. Witnessing a car accident or traumatic event can instill intense fear, allowing a spirit of fear to enter and perpetuate ongoing fearfulness and even PTSD.

Action List: make a list of (1) all abuse and traumatic events (either personal or observed), (2) any sinful emotions or responses occurring as a result of each event, and (3) the people directly involved (if applicable) with those events.

_____

_____

_____

_____

_____

#11 Addictions

Addictions, such as drugs, alcohol, pornography, and sex, are sins that can open doors for unholy spirits to intensify and incite more of that same behavior. Often, many of these spirits of addiction originally entered through unholy soul ties between you and the first people who introduced you to those activities. For example, if you have a drug addiction, these soul ties could be the first people who introduced you to prescription drugs that eventually led you to illegal drugs (this could be a first grade teacher who suggested you had ADHD, the physician to prescribed medication for ADHD, and your mother who forced you to take the medication). Or it could be the friends who encouraged you to try a certain drug and you got addicted. If you have a smoking addiction, it may be the person who taught you to smoke and gave you your first pack of cigarettes. In other words, *all* people who were involved with your initial encounters that ultimately led to your addiction are crucial to write on this list.

Action List: make a list of (1) all addictions, (2) those involved with your initial encounters that started your addiction journey, (3) who you have ever bought supplies from (ex. who you got drugs from), and (4) who you have done those addictions with (ex. who you partied with). If you have suffered with addictions for a long time, your list may be extensive. If you do not recall specific names, describe the individuals (ex. "guy with the blue hat"). If you don't remember *everyone*, ask the Lord to remind you of those you need to list in order to remove the legal rights from the tormenting spirits.

_____

_____

_____

_____

_____

_____

_____

#12 Other Religions
Engaging in worship or acts of honoring, praying to, or worshipping gods of other religions can create open doors for torment. Worship means engaging in *any* activity, however small you may feel it was.

Action list: make a list of any religions you, your parents, or your ancestors have engaged in, regardless of how minor or insignificant the involvement may have been. List the person and religion, and any spirit names, if known. If the Lord seems to place something in your mind that seems unlikely, write it down. If you're wrong, it won't hurt to repent of it. If you're right, it might help set you free.

_____

_____

_____

_____

#13 Other Sins

"Other sins" are any other sins the Lord brings to mind that do not fit into the previous categories. For instance, if you knowingly went against the Lord's instruction, such as taking a medication or health treatment he specifically advised against, that action would be considered a sin. Or, since your body is the Temple of God, if you consistently eat foods or participate in unhealthy activities, that may be considered a sin. Or, if you have had an abortion, performed an abortion, or encouraged someone to get an abortion, that, too, is sin. Or, if an attitude of resentment towards God has crept into your heart, that, too, is sin.

Action list: make a list of any additional sins you have not placed on a list yet, including anything the Lord reveals you are doing to your body that is not healthy, any entertainment you engage in the Lord prompts you to stop (books, music, movies), or anything else you've done that he brings to mind

_____

_____

_____

_____

_____

_____

_____

#14 Agreement Sins

An "agreement sin" refers to the act of you or an ancestor agreeing to oaths, rituals, or any other type of agreement that is contrary to God. This often occurs both with groups that use secret oaths (such as Shriners, Freemasons, and even the Mormon Church's "penalty" oath prior to 1990), and with occult practices such as witchcraft, Wicca, any form of divination (tarot cards, palm reading, use of water or mineral divining rods, etc), or Luciferian organizations. Any occultic activity you, or an ancestor, have participated in (see list in "List #5 Occult" description above) is usually tied to agreement sins.

Action list: make a list of (1) any <u>secret oath groups</u> you, a parent, or any ancestor may have participated in; list the person and the group if known; (2) any <u>occultic activity</u> either you, or an ancestor, have participated in; list the person and the occult practice if known; and (3) any <u>other type of agreement or iniquity sins</u> you are aware of from any ancestor (slavery, murder [including abortion], adultery, etc.).

_____

_____

_____

_____

_____

#15 Infirmity

An infirmity is any form of sickness, disease, or ailment you would normally go to the doctor to seek help for. Infirmities could be things such as: **family illnesses, premature death in your family, arthritis, allergies, asthma, cancer, heart disease, circulatory/vascular issues, infertility, any type of "disorder," any type of "syndrome," chronic pain, or anything else.** While infirmities are not sins, they may be *tied* to sins. The purpose of listing any infirmities is to specifically ask the Lord to remove them from you.

Action list: make a list of any infirmities you have, or any infirmities you see as patterns in your family line.

_____

_____

_____

_____

_____

#16 Additional Sins and Issues

While many people have committed some of the sins listed below at some point in their life, the purpose of this list is to identify those sins or issues that are **consistently present** in your life. Anytime a sin or issue is *consistently* present, it may be an indication that an unholy spirit is involved.

Action list: mark each item below that you struggle with as a "strong urge" in your life *when* it appears.

(The following list is © Above and Beyond Christian Counseling. Visit their website for more information at: AandBCounseling.com).

HAUGHTY
Pride / Vanity
Perfection
Accusation / Scorn
Judgmental / Condemning
Self-Judgmental / Self-Condemning
Competition
Mockery
Stubbornness
Selfishness
Gossip
Boastful
Self-righteousness Embarrassment / Humiliation
Sarcasm
Critical

DEAF & DUMB
Mental Illness / Insanity
Double Mindedness
Seizures / Epilepsy
Mind binding
Stupor

SLUMBER
Isolation / Anti-social
Sleepiness / Laziness
Forgetfulness
Stupidity
Daydreaming/Trances
Apathy / Indifference
Confusion

HEAVINESS
Misery / Dread
Rejection / Self-rejection
Despair / Hopelessness
Grief
Fatigue / Weariness
Guilt / Shame
Self-pity
Loneliness
Depression / Manic Depression
Suicide / Death

FEAR
Insecurity / Inadequacy /
Inferiority
Timidity
Worry / Anxiety
Fear of Death
Cowardice / Cowering
Hiding / Escaping
Fear of Authority / Speaking
Fear of Being Abused
Terror / Torment
Nightmares
Panic Attacks
Phobias (_____)
Nervousness / Hyperactivity /
Unrest
Abandonment
Future / Failure

Little girl / boy personality spirits

JEALOUSY
Impatience / Frustration
Bitterness / Negativity / Blaming
Strife / Division / Conflict
Envy / Covetousness
Control / Manipulation
Revenge / Retaliation
Suspicion
Anger / Rage
Hatred / Self-hatred
Cruelty
Murder / Violence
Murmuring / Complaining
Profanity

LYING
Exaggeration / Drama
Hypocrisy Religious / Legalism / Tradition
Word Twisting
Theft
ANTI-CHRIST
Doubt & Unbelief
Rebellion
Humanism / Intellectualism
Self-help
Self-exaltation

WHOREDOM
Worldliness
Idolatry
Fornication
Adultery

PERVERSION
Lust
Homosexuality / Les-
   bianism
Gender Dysphoria

Prostitution / Mastur-
   bation
Sodomy
Bestiality
Molestation / Incest
Exhibitionism
Pornography

Seducing Spirit
Fantasy Spirits
Incubus / Succubus
Sensual Thoughts
Other_____

POVERTY

BONDAGE
Hindering / Distrac-
   tion Greed /
   Hoarding
Gluttony
Slavery / Emotional
   Weakness
Addiction
   (_____)
Other
   (_____)

ABOUT THE AUTHOR

Beatty Carmichael is a Christian business owner called to be a full-time minister serving the business community.

He is a gifted Bible teacher who teaches deep, complex truths in an easy-to-understand way. His teaching content can be found on his podcast channel, Get Radical Faith, and on the internet at GetRadicalFaith.com.

As a business owner, he is a marketing professional specializing in helping real estate agents in the U.S.A. get more listings. His company and services can be found at AgentDominator.com.

Made in the USA
Columbia, SC
25 October 2023